NOTM
SA

UNTO THE ALTAR

UNTO THE ALTAR

THE PRACTICE
OF CATHOLIC WORSHIP

EDITED BY
ALFONS KIRCHGAESSNER

HERDER AND HERDER

1963
HERDER AND HERDER NEW YORK
232 Madison Avenue, New York 16, N. Y.

Original edition "Unser Gottesdienst", Herder, Freiburg
Translated by Rosaleen Brennan

Library of Congress Catalog Card Number: 62-19566
First published in West Germany © 1963 Herder KG
Printed in West Germany by Herder

"IN THE FREQUENT CONVERSE OF
OUR HEART WITH THE CHRISTIAN PEOPLE
WE ALWAYS RECALL A SAYING
OF ONE OF THE GREATEST OF RELIGIOUS
THINKERS, BOSSUET:
'THERE IS NO FULFILMENT IN
RELIGIOUS WORK AND IN CHRISTIAN LIFE
EXCEPT IN PARTICIPATION IN THE
EUCHARISTIC MEAL.'
TO THIS PARTICIPATION OUGHT TO BE
DEDICATED THE WHOLE ENDEAVOUR
OF PASTORAL CONCERNS . . .
IT IS FROM THE ALTAR, FROM THIS
HOLY MOUNT, THAT WE MUST VIEW,
JUDGE AND MAKE USE OF
THE THINGS OF THIS WORLD.
EVEN THE MOST DIFFICULT QUESTIONS
IN THE LIVES OF MEN MUST HERE
FIND THEIR POINT OF
DEPARTURE FOR A JUST SOLUTION."

From an Address of Pope John XXIII.
on November 23, 1958, on the occasion of taking possession
of the Lateran Basilica.

Contents

Foreword

1963 MARKS the sixtieth birthday of the present "Liturgical Movement". When men in high and low places no longer saw in the Church's liturgy the foremost fountain of divine worship and the primary source of full life in Christ; when the realization that the eucharistic Sacrifice, the sacraments and the sacramentals are, indeed, the highest expression of that honor which individuals and the community owe to the majesty of God and, at the same time, constitute the deepest mainspring of sanctification of the human family, had reached its lowest ebb, the Spirit of God touched the heart of the great Pius X, with the *ignis ardens,* the "fire burning" for the restoration of the divine cult. With celestial vision which Pius possessed in no small measure, he quickly responded to the *motu proprio* of the Holy Spirit by issuing his *Motu proprio* for the purpose of leading the Christian world back to the fountains of the true Christian spirit. Already three months after his elevation to the chair of Peter, Pius sent forth this immortal clarion-call: "Active participation in the sacred mysteries and the solemn prayers of the Church is the primary and indispensable source of the true Christian spirit" (November 22, 1903).

A sower went out to sow ... but some of the precious seed fell by the wayside, some on the rubble and other some among

9

the thorns. Six, seven years later, some of it began to sprout, first in Belgium, then in France and Germany, and, some twenty years later, in the United States. Sixty years have elapsed since the birth of this "movement" toward the fountains of the true Christian spirit. Would the urgent, paternal call of Pope John "for the renewal of the Church" have been so necessary if clergy and laity had listened to the voice of Pius X sixty years ago? Would we not rather witness in many parts of the world a great flourishing of the "true Christian spirit" if sixty years ago all of us, old and young, high and low, clergy and faithful, had humbly and honestly begun their march toward the "primary (!) and indispensable (!) source" of that true Christian spirit, which means the very life and love of Christ the Savior?

I make bold to say that in the United States less than thirty percent of the forty-eight millions of Catholics have thus far been touched by the "burning fire" of St. Pius X; by that foremost and indispensable fountain whence flows "the abundant life" which the Savior offered to the world. True, some noteworthy efforts have been made, particularly since the *"Instructio"* of 1958, but I am afraid that two-thirds of the so-called "active" participants have not risen much above mere "external" participation. To put it in an everyday example: A once rusty wire has been neatly polished, but the current is still wanting. *Cor et vox,* heart and voice must go together. Only then can we speak of "active participation". Thus we are urged to give interior effect to our outward observance, otherwise religion clearly amounts to "mere formalism" (*Mediator Dei* 24).

Let us not say that all of this is due to the absence of "vernacular". Certainly, the use of the vernacular can be helpful, but it surely is no cure-all. Or, do we recite the rosary so much

10

more fervently because we are doing it in the vernacular? Unless I understand the meaning and spirit of the "fifteen mysteries" and have some idea on how to meditate on them, it would make little difference whether I say the rosary in English, in Latin or even in Chinese. If "faith comes from hearing", then growth and perfection of the true Christian spirit comes from an intelligent and soulful contact with the fountain whence it flows. No wonder that Pius XII made this poignant remark: "We earnestly exhort you to promote a deeper knowledge of the liturgy among the people, so that they may more readily and easily follow the sacred rites and take part in them with true Christian dispositions" (*Mediator Dei*, 186).

One wonders if the spirit of St. Pius X did not hover with pentecostal power over the first session of the Holy Council, the II Vatican, when the Fathers of the Council decided, contrary to original plans, to take up for their first "schema" the sacred liturgy, directing their special attention to these important chapters: 1) The nature of the liturgy, its meaning to the Church for her mission and for the spiritual life of her members. 2) The promotion of liturgical formation and the active participation by the faithful. 3) The structure of the liturgy with special emphasis on its pastoral and communal function. 4) The furtherance of the liturgy in diocese and parish. 5) The promotion of the liturgical apostolate in "glad tidings that shall be to all the people", hopeful signs of better things to come for the renewal of the Church, and the long overdue ripening of the precious seed planted by the great Pius sixty years ago.

Just because faithful and clergy have been all too long and all too far away from the enkindling fire of the liturgy, it is of great importance that priests with the "earnestness", urged by Pius XII, cultivate in their own minds and hearts "a deeper knowledge of the liturgy", celebrate with greater reverence, free from all haste, the living and life-imparting mysteries: the Holy Sacrifice, the sacraments, the sacramentals and the divine office and then, with charismatic conviction and holy zeal, so teach and guide their flock "that they may more readily and easily follow the sacred rites and take part in them with true Christian dispositions".

We owe a debt of gratitude to Father Alfons Kirchgaessner for the precious "mosaic" which he, together with fifteen other leaders, presents to clergy and laity alike. I have been greatly inspired by the pages of this thought-provoking work. In fact, I consider the 22 chapters of this book as a pastoral "yes" to the above-mentioned five chapters of the Council's "schema" on the sacred liturgy. Surely, the more earnestly and wholeheartedly shepherds and flock will take in the rich contents of this most welcome book, the more they will be drawn "unto the altar" where heaven and earth embrace each other and where "Jesus manifests His glory and His disciples believe in Him".

Epiphany, 1963

MARTIN B. HELLRIEGEL, M. A., L. H. D.

1

Some Dangers of the Liturgical Revival

Romano Guardini

ALL life's manifestations have their particular strong points and potentialities, as also their dangers and weaknesses. In the present attempt to examine the liturgical question, I wish to indicate a series of dangers which have become apparent in the course of time. This cannot be done without using certain labels. These are, of course, hardly commendable, since they easily distort the matter under discussion; but I do not see how they could be avoided. So I am indicating in advance the concomitant disadvantages.

I should, in fact, like to begin with the danger which appeared first, namely Rubricism.

By this I mean the tendency to attribute to the liturgy an importance which it does not possess. Such an inclination is understandable. It is always found when something important has for a long time had insufficient attention paid to it and is now, as it were, discovered anew. Enthusiasm is aroused; work, time and money are devoted to it; discussion begins; and the discovery is automatically over-rated. Forgetting that the Catholic Christian religious life has other forms, people have frequently regarded the liturgy as its only one. The monastic community with its special conditions has been taken as the prototype of the Christian community in general and so the limits,

13

which there are to liturgical work in a parish, have not been realized. Sometimes there has been no understanding at all of how this community really lives, of what are its religious needs and potentialities and what its particular problems etc. The result of all this has been something forced and exaggerated, made more acute by an emphatically aesthetic way of thought and feeling, which ignores the difficulties and duties of real life and gives an undesirable character to the whole liturgical endeavour.

So occasionally there appeared beside the real, essential and fruitful conceptions of liturgical life an ideal image which bore no relation to reality. Its advocates demanded that the Latin plainchant be used for congregational singing; they failed to recognize the importance of popular devotion, as expressed in the Stations of the Cross, the Rosary and the different words of the hymnals; they underestimated the value of hymn-singing; they did not take into account the individual nature of the personal life of prayer, and so on. If, however, an exaggeration among the originators is serious, how much more so among their followers and their followers' adherents – particularly when it is a matter of people substituting clichés for genuine work and false zeal for true enthusiasm.

At the other extreme is an attitude which is called Activism. The word is particularly ugly, but I know no better.

The tendency I have just described exaggerated the importance of the liturgy. It had forgotten the saying that "the Sabbath is made for man" and if it also, and rightly, was able to stress that for a truly spiritual and religious life nothing is more important than that things should be done purely for their own sake (which in this context means for the glory of God), it nevertheless failed to recognize the needs of daily life. The advocates

14

of practice could therefore point with justified emphasis to all the shortcomings which resulted from Rubricism – but meanwhile erred themselves by going to the opposite extreme.

Activism arose from the confrontation between the work of the Church and the needs of modern life, the social and economic factors which beset it, and the consequent moral problems. It was intended to help people overcome the new situation in a Christian way. For this reason it transferred the focus of pastoral activity entirely to organization and teaching and saw the value of ecclesiastical things, including public worship, in the serving of these practical ends. In doing this it frequently failed to appreciate the essence of the religious life, its inner meaning and its dignity, which cannot be subordinated to any such ends. At times it went so far as to feel that prayer, the undemanding absorption of self in eternal things, the sacred worship before God's countenance, was a waste of time.

All this led to regarding the liturgy as something pointless and superfluous – and hence it was suppressed in favour of spiritual methods and forms of worship apparently more up-to-date and effective; or it was refashioned with a view to achieving moral or other stimulating effects. In this way Activism failed to recognize the original and most important meaning of the liturgy; at the same time it destroyed for the sake of immediate results an irreplaceable tool of pastoral work. For the fewer the intentions associated with it, the more blessings the liturgy brings. It is a steady light, constantly burning; a gentle flame, continually warming; a force, silently at work, moulding and purifying. As such it needs the peace and freedom to develop, unhampered by aims and motives, and if these are provided, it can create a foundation which supports anything and an order

15

which makes its influence felt everywhere. This is what has been overlooked by Activism. Harried by the difficulties of present-day life, Activism has looked for quick, immediate, even numerically tangible results and therefore neglected one of the most important means of fruitful, penetrating and, above all, lasting activity.

These two tendencies I have described have been with us for a long time; a third is of more recent origin. I should like to call it liturgical Dilettantism.

When any fundamentally good endeavour has been operative for some time, the moment always comes when it makes a sudden leap into the awareness of the general public. While previously it had to assert itself laboriously, all at once it becomes a contemporary issue – an important but dangerous moment, because it brings with it the threat of hasty, disjointed, and insufficiently experienced action. For liturgical work that moment has come. Its importance has dawned on many, clergy and laity alike, especially, as one would expect, among the younger generation; and now something has appeared which, though well-intentioned in itself, is often disastrous in its effects. The importance of genuine spirituality for the life of the parish has been accepted and since it has been recognized that its mainspring lies in the liturgy, a start has been made on the liturgical refashioning of public worship. At the same time there has been an attempt to bring the worship of the parish nearer to the reality of daily life. All this, however, is frequently done by those who lack the required ability for this task and who do not bring to it the necessary prudence.

Following from the idea that a man can only pray in his native language, the use of the vernacular was stressed. Out of

16

a conviction of the importance of liturgical symbols came the attempt to lay greater stress on them and to give the sacred ceremonies a more popular character. Attempts were made to create what is with more or less justice called a popular liturgy. In all this there was much which was not only well-meant but also correct in its approach; at the same time, however, disastrous inadequacies were revealed. Above all, the attempts made were often unconnected and arbitrary ones, varying in form from place to place, so that confusions perforce arose. Often the most elementary prerequisites were lacking. Many of those who ventured into this field had no conception of the amount of historical, theological, philological and musical knowledge required to bring out more clearly the essence of a symbolic action or to compose a tune which is both in the tradition of plainchant and truly part of the life of the people. Indeed at times it was apparent that their knowledge not only of Latin but even of their own language was inadequate.

In addition, it was disastrous that other questions of a different nature should come to be associated with the liturgical movement; for example, uninformed conceptions of the place of the laity in the Church, or about the relationship between ethical and spiritual values, and so on. The opposition between older and younger generations played its part in this too. Strained relations between parish-priest and curate or between the priests of different parishes undoubtedly made themselves felt—as did all the other things which are brought into play in matters of this sort by the muddleheadedness of human beings. Very awkward situations have often been the result.

Thus the conditions were favourable for a fourth tendency, which I should like to call liturgical Conservatism.

This is, in itself, a fundamental human emotion, which constantly asserts itself in history, taking on a particular character according to the varying nature of the age and the aspirations which it is opposing. In this case, the liturgical Conservatives felt keenly the dangers I have just set out. They saw that Rubricism did not take into account the real nature of parish life, while Dilettantism brought the danger of confusion and arbitrary action. In opposition to Activism, they stressed the necessity to build upon the inner basic religious life, rather than in external methods and aids. In all this they were right, but they fell into the danger of rejecting anything to which they were not accustomed.

As far as they are concerned, "traditional" equals "good" and "new" equals "irreligious". As soon as someone does something other than what has always been done, they regard it as evidence of a revolutionary spirit. They often do not consider how the matter really stands. Perhaps what is being abandoned by the person they are criticizing, had originated in the spiritually most unproductive years of the nineteenth century and had in its time ousted some precious devotional heritage of the Church. Above all they overlook the fact that the liturgy is far from taking the place which is its due in the life of the parish. Popular and private devotions, sometimes of very doubtful value, often fill out the spiritual life of the parish, and liturgical ceremonies of the highest importance are brushed aside, so that irreplaceable opportunities for pastoral care are lost. The celebration of Holy Mass itself has in many cases come to resemble a popular devotion in character. Any variety in the life of public worship has now widely disappeared and been replaced by an inner monotony, the disastrous effects of which have been nowhere near sufficiently realized. The practice of the sacraments has been removed and alienated from its essential context; on this subject a great deal could be said.

The liturgical Conservatives stress that one thing is too elevated for the ordinary people and another too unfamiliar; it is, however, very doubtful whether they have seriously tried to educate the people. They say that women cannot understand certain liturgical practices and that men need an ostensibly stronger religious diet; it remains, however, very much a question which men and women have expressed these opinions; and equally, whether a really serious and devoted attempt has been made to awaken men's minds to the great pattern of the liturgy and women's feelings for its deep and joyful mystery.

Nor are they so familiar with the real spiritual needs of the faithful, particularly of the younger ones, as one might suppose from hearing them constantly emphasizing their experience. Otherwise they would realize that people are driven from the church by having outmoded forms of worship forced upon them and that liturgy for many people, and especially the young, is quite simply one of life's necessities. If they are told this, however, they only talk of the pride of intellectuals and the arrogance of the young, who always want to have something out of the ordinary.

Indeed at times the stern judges of liturgical endeavours have themselves no precise idea of what in fact liturgy is. I should like to recall, and not simply as barren criticism, how inadequate the liturgical education of the clergy often was; the liturgy has for a long time belonged to those subjects which were treated rather as poor relations, grouped together under the general concept "pastoral theology". So it is understandable if many of them imagine the liturgy as something which is simply there, but the fundamental meaning of which cannot be comprehended. Given, in addition, the awkward situations described above, one is forced to admit that, from a subjective point of view, the conservatives are technically correct in their fight against liturgical efforts, for it is really very doubtful what they understand by the word – they certainly do not mean the true liturgy of the Church.

I have tried to present four points at which the difficulty of the liturgical situation is revealed. I share and respect the scruples of the responsible authorities and should like to express a further anxiety, which refers directly to them, namely, the danger of an administrative short-circuit.

The Church authorities are responsible for the ordering of religious life. Therefore they are justifiably suspicious of arbitrary action and lack of discipline, of anything out-of-the-way or artificial. This fact leads to anxieties lest, faced with the present situation, they should want to create order at any price and in so doing put an end to good and important endeavours. Having been concerned with liturgical work for over thirty-five years, I think I can see the importance of the matters under discussion. I know many of those who are working on them, I know how much love and labour they have devoted to them, simply out of loyalty to the Church, a loyalty which cannot be doubted in them any more than in another fallible human being. I believe, moreover, that the time in which we are living is of the greatest significance not only for the external but also for the inner history of the Church, and it will not be easy in the future to put right what is being neglected or done badly.

Not everything is possible in every age – how important then that what is necessary now should be done in a proper manner.

It is natural that the ecclesiastical authorities should take steps against arbitrary innovations, justified neither by office nor by ability. It is more than just that they should demand and require caution from their priests, especially the younger ones, and that the latter should have to learn before they act on their own account. On the other hand a great deal depends on them, not to withdraw their confidence from those who have been working on these matters for so long with seriousness and feelings of responsibility, but to protect them from attacks which call in question their convictions and their work.

What any liturgical work needs is time. There is a lot to do, the problems are great. To make progress, much theoretical knowledge, much practical knowledge, manifold linguistic and musical abilities are necessary. So we ask for patience. We know that it is asking a great deal to leave things in the balance. But otherwise no good can come of it; and measures which would hinder a work, already several decades old, from yielding matured fruits, would be far worse than any temporary uncertainty.

In recent years attacks have been made which have found a strong response. They have certainly arisen from honest concern, and my own exposition has in fact shown that there is good cause for it. We trust, however, in the wisdom and justice of our bishops, that they will not value these criticisms more highly than their truth warrants. It would be easy to list the disadvantages of the pastoral methods advocated by our critics, which are just as bad as those censured by them; mistakes are regrettable; ultimately, however, it is not a question of mistakes

21

but of the true underlying motives. When have good ideas not been abused? What would our opponents say if there were cited against what they advocate all the true and real facts that are to be found in life and literature? They would be indignant. They would demand that their ideas be discussed in their pure and genuine form; they would say that it was unfair to approach an intellectual position through its weak or minor points – and they would be right. May they themselves do likewise! I know enough of theory and practice to be able to answer them in a way they could not ignore, but I do not wish to do so. I turn rather to our bishops, full of confidence, and convinced that they will distinguish true from false, essential from inessential, lasting from transient, and that they will not permit an easily inflammable atmosphere to call in question the honour and the fruits of decades of work . . .

2

Mass Intentions and Mass Stipends

J. A. JUNGMANN S. J.

IT IS our custom today to associate a definite intention with every celebration of the Mass: it is offered for someone or for some purpose. Usually a Mass-stipend is taken for it. When on Sundays and Holy Days the parish-priest is not permitted to accept any stipend, since he has to "apply" the Mass to the needs of the parish, we feel this is something of an exception, which we can, however, justify in so far as the stipend for the Mass is, in fact, included in his salary or his benefice.

At the same time we cannot deceive ourselves: we feel a certain uneasiness about this custom and its usual explanation. And this feeling increases the more vividly we have in our minds an ideal picture of the celebration of the Eucharist, an ideal which the new liturgical fervour has awakened in us, of the Eucharist as the memorial of the Lord, the sacrifice of the New Covenant, offered in thanksgiving among the communion of the faithful, who in this way present their whole lives to God and return to everyday life strengthened once more by the Bread of Life. How can we reconcile intention and stipend with this concept?

We sense, too, that our uneasiness is not without cause, since there is scarcely a treatise on Mass-stipends which does not contain passages dismissing in more or less detail the suspicion of simony. For it is a fact that money is given if not for the Mass, then for the fruits which the donor of the stipend expects from the Mass celebrated for him *(fructus specialis or ministerialis)*. Various solutions have been propounded by canon lawyers to avoid this reproach. They say, for example, that "stipend", as the word suggests, implies only a contribution to the support we owe our pastors, or that the gift is to be understood as alms *(eleemosynae missarum),* or that it is only the time and effort expended which is rewarded, not the spiritual act. But with such answers we provide only an excuse for something which looks like a necessary evil. Should then the whole system of Mass-stipends be banned from the Church, as the representatives of eighteenth-century Enlightenment demanded (cp. 1530). Or is there, in fact, a more positive view of this custom which the Church has preserved?

First of all it must be said that it is by no means in the nature of the Mass that it should be applied to a definite intention; for it is meaningful in itself without any special intention. In the Sunday worship of the assembled community we have the fundamental form of the Eucharistic celebration. For centuries the Sunday Mass stood so much in the foreground that other customs were scarcely mentioned, indeed to a large extent did not exist at all. On Sunday everyone assembled to do what the Lord commanded his Church to do: to renew his commemoration, to thank God for all the great things that he has given us in his creation and, above all, in his Son, and to associate our thanks with the perpetual sacrifice which renews Christ himself in our midst.

Thanksgiving was so central to this worship that the exhortation which immediately precedes the beginning of the sacred actions runs: *Gratias agamus Domino Deo nostro.* The celebration

24

itself was for a long time simply called *"Eucharistia"* and from this the sacrament, too, took its name. Even if, in more precise terms, we speak of "the sacrifice", the tone remains fundamentally the same; the sacrifice is indeed the gift with which we pay our homage, with which we confess God as Lord of all things. It is this original function of the Eucharistic celebration which underlies the fact that today the parish-priest is still bound to celebrate the sacrifice on Sundays and Holy Days of Obligation as head of his parish. "To apply it to the parish" is a less satisfactory expression; it merely implies that there is no question of private application here and recognizes simply the first and most essential function of the celebration of Mass: the adoration and homage of God's people to God, our Lord.

But the Mass is not only thanksgiving and adoration. Since in the New Covenant it is the only sacrifice, it is at the same time a sacrifice of atonement and of intercession. For this reason it has from earliest times been offered for special intentions, for a particular *votum* (Votive Masses). The account given in the apocryphal, half-gnostic Acts of John, written around the middle of the second century, of the Apostle John standing by a tomb, breaking the bread, beginning a prayer of thanksgiving and then distributing the Eucharist to those gathered around the grave, clearly mirrors a custom extant even at that time in the Catholic Church: the celebration of the Eucharist for the dead. A little later this custom is, in fact, attested by Tertullian: *Oblationes pro defunctis . . . annua die facimus* (De cor. ch. 3). We have frequent proofs of the fact that the Eucharist was also occasionally celebrated for a small group in a private house or chapel, and then, too, probably for a special intention. In the *Gelasian*

25

Sacramentary (the Roman Missal which dates in its essentials from the sixth century) the whole of the third part, after the Proper of the Day and the Proper of the Saints, is composed almost exclusively of formularies for Votive Masses. In the three variable prayers and often in the *Hanc Igitur* as well, there are more or less precise references to particular intentions which are stated in the titles: help in any trouble, in danger of plague; prayer for rain, for fine weather, for the blessing of children, for the sick, for the dead, in time of war, for peace; thanks and prayers for a birthday, at a marriage, on the anniversary of a priest's ordination, etc.

Since the third century it has become more and more the practice for the faithful to express their bond with the altar by bringing first bread and wine and later other gifts, for the needs of the Church and the priest, to Mass as their offering. This practice was also observed at Votive Masses. Augustine (*Ep.* 111. 8) laments the fate of Christian women who have fallen into the power of the heathen and can no longer find a priest *"per quem offerant Deo"*. Gregory of Tours (d. 594), that inexhaustible storyteller, has preserved for us an anecdote which gives a particularly vivid illustration of this custom. (*De gloria conf.* ch. 65). For a whole year a widow had the sacrifice offered daily for her dead husband and would bring with her each time a measure of the best wine, which, according to Gallic custom, she would hand into the sacristy. Since the woman did not, however, go to communion every day, the unscrupulous subdeacon who served the priest at Mass and who, at the Offertory, had to carry the wine-offering from the sacristy to the altar carried out this fraud: he took the good wine for himself and substituted for it cheap, sour wine, until finally the woman communicated again and discovered the deception. The offering on the part of the faithful was, therefore, quite simply implicit in the Mass. The Offertory procession has, significantly enough, been retained in many places up to the present day in what are (in the original sense already mentioned) Votive Masses, in so far as they concern a small section of the faithful: for example, Requiem Masses, Nuptial Masses, and the annual services of a guild or confraternity. Formerly the whole congregation would take part in an Offertory procession on Sundays and Holy Days as well, a practice which was, as is well known, made compulsory by Gregory VII when it threatened to lapse.

The essential nature of the practice was in no way altered by the fact that gifts in kind were increasingly replaced by money, even though the symbolism became less obvious as a result. The symbolism was further weakened, although again without a change in its essential nature, when, in the case of the private offering, the presentation of the gift took place separately from the liturgical proceedings. We even find this, although here it is an exception, in the early days of Christianity, where it is the handing over of a gift of money before the liturgical action: Epiphanius, for example, records of a newly-baptized person that he handed a sum of money to the bishop who baptized him with the request: Make an offering for me! (*Adv. Haer.* 30:6)

In the later Middle Ages it became more and more the general custom to give the priest a gift beforehand. Even when the Mass in question already had a definite intention and perhaps already contained an Offertory procession (say, on behalf of a family who had asked for the Mass), anyone could include himself in the Mass, according to the current practice, through a gift

27

given beforehand or through joining in the Offertory procession. Frequently, as a result of this, there was even a second Offertory procession at the beginning of the Mass. It was called – quite without embarrassment – buying oneself into the Mass: *comparare Missam*. This *comparatio Missae* was already present, in a narrower sense, if the priest was offered a gift to oblige him to celebrate Mass for the sole intention of the donor. This is the Mass-stipend in the narrow sense. The exclusiveness of the principle in force today, that only one stipend may be taken for each Mass, is not an inevitable consequence following from the very nature of the matter, but goes back to a well-founded rule of canon law from Urban VIII's Constitutio, *"Cum saepe"*, of 1625. For since the intercessory power of the Sacrifice of the Mass, which is in fact that of the Sacrifice of the Cross, as the majority of theologians maintain, is in itself unlimited and can only be limited by the receptiveness of the recipient, it can, therefore, be applied to more than one intention at the same time. The axiom *"Intentio non excludit intentionem"* is just as valid as the axiom *"Stipendium excludit stipendium"* (K. Rahner).

What happens then when the priest accepts a stipend from someone and then celebrates according to the wish of the donor? The same thing happens as when formerly the priest accepted the gift of bread and wine from someone within the action of the Mass and the donor participated in this expressive way in the offering of the sacrifice. The donor's gift is not offered to the priest himself but is a sacrificial gift to God; it is accepted by the priest and administered by him on God's behalf, the priest having the right to dispose of what remains after the offering. He is God's trustee. Hence the canon-lawyer

28

Klaus Mörsdorf defines the Mass-stipend as "a gift entrusted to the priest's keeping to be used for the Holy Sacrifice of the Mass and which on the completion of the Sacrifice comes to the priest from the altar as a gratuitous gift".

This conception of the Mass-stipend, which has been brought into repute again in our day by Fr. Maurice de la Taille, has of course certain consequences. A stipend can only be accepted from one who can participate in the sacrifice, that is, from a baptized person who enjoys full membership of the Church. In the early days of the Church this rule was very strictly interpreted. The offerings of all those who lived openly in sin like usurers and prostitutes were to be refused. Indeed even penitents could not regain the right of presenting their gift until after their reconciliation. Heretics and unbaptized persons were even more firmly excluded.

This conception was adhered to on principle throughout the Middle Ages. Even according to the present law the Mass cannot be publicly offered for excommunicated persons (can. 1241 2262). On the other hand, there are Roman decisions issued in the nineteenth century which permit the acceptance of a stipend from unbelievers. The basis here is no longer the true concept of a stipend but a concept which looks upon it more as a gift to the priest (eleemosynae) and no longer takes into account the connection with the altar. Here, too, there is no question of a theological ruling but of a decision of canon law, in which alms from the hand of an unbaptized person and prayer for him are declared admissible. From the theological view the Mass-stipend remains an offering to God, made by someone entitled to do so by virtue of his participation in the priesthood of Christ given him at baptism, and as a member of his Church.

It is to this conception of the gift in the practice of Mass-stipends that we should, if possible, once again give weight as part of our pastoral duties. This means that, where possible, the donor of the stipend should take part in "his" Mass by being present in person, and also that he should be informed of the day and hour of his Mass, as is, indeed, the general practice in parishes. If, because the stipends are passed on, the celebrating priest is only aware of a number, as may sometimes be unavoidable, the resulting weakening of one of the spiritual values is, nevertheless, to be regretted. For the donor can justly expect and desire that the priest should celebrate the sacrifice, which he is offering on his behalf, in inner sympathy with his intentions and should thus help him to secure acceptance and hearing with God.

Apart from this it is definitely a false application of commercial ideas to a sphere where there is a *commercium* of a quite different sort, if it is thought that at each Mass the priest can dispose of a certain number of benefits, to be conferred at his discretion, and that he has to confer them by his own act if the celebration is not to be valueless. Rather is it correct to say: the priest need only offer the sacrifice as the one in which the donor has a share through his stipend; the benefit is then automatically conferred.

Moreover, the first object of the celebration of the Mass, as has already been indicated, is far from being that of gaining a specific benefit for someone or something in particular. That is a secondary function which first came to light in the case of what has been called up till now the "private Mass", the Votive Mass, that is, one which arises from a particular votum, and even here only as a provision that when he celebrates in private the priest will not celebrate primarily from his own motives and in his own spiritual interests. Still less can the application of the stipend be of primary interest when the Mass takes place with a fairly large congregation; for then those present, who simply wish to sanctify their day's work through their participation in this sacrifice of the Mass, are in the first instance the co-offerers of the sacrifice and, pre-supposing an appropriate devotion, are so in at least the same degree as the donor of the stipend, if he is not, in fact, present himself. This leads, for example, to the conclusion that in the case of frequently recurring Masses for the Dead the celebrant does better, in the interest of those present and participating, to follow the general Calendar in choosing the Proper.

3

Personal Prayer and the Prayers of the Church

Romano Guardini

Personal Prayer

Personal prayer corresponds very closely to the human beings who practise it, since it is the expression of their inmost being; it is the more perfect, the stronger and purer it is. Thus the way in which one person prays is not necessarily suitable for others. It is true that everyone includes other people in his prayers: relations, friends, those in need. The more unselfish a man becomes, the further his concerns and his prayers extend; yet, when all is said and done, he is alone with God. That saying, which originated among the first hermits in the Egyptian desert and was coined anew by Augustine and restated by Cardinal Newman, is still valid in this context: "God and my soul, nothing else." Personal prayer belongs to that holy inner solitude which encompasses God and the individual and encompasses them anew each time. God does not regard men in the mass. He treats each one as though there were no others.

Personal prayer is subject to definite laws: revealed doctrines such as are to be found in Holy Scripture, rules of Christian experience such as have been worked out in the tradition of the Church, and standards of prudence and good sense which are as valid for prayer as for any other intellectual activity. Nevertheless, personal prayer is free in a special sense. It is indeed possible to speak of rules and regulations concerning it, for, like all living things, it can only thrive within an ordered framework. Yet these are but a protection; in its essential nature personal prayer has its origin in a direct impulse of the heart. The more vital it is, the less rules of behaviour can be imposed on it; rather, it will change according to a man's inner state, according to his experiences and the circumstances in which he finds himself. This freedom is a fundamental element of prayer. When it is not given, prayer becomes drab, hesitating and lacking in vigour. Education in personal prayer must, therefore, make the growth and development of prayer a fundamental and well-established part of it. Even personal prayer is a duty. It does not spring – at least not ideally – from necessity but from truth. It is not the mere expression of the individual soul but the performing of what is right. If it were merely self-expression, it would become undisciplined and unfruitful. Nevertheless, freedom is part of its nature. It is a service which has only one purpose: that man should seek not himself, but God; that he should not follow the dictates of his own heart, but remain within the limits of truth and order. In other respects personal prayer is a voluntary service, regulated only by willingness and generosity.

The Liturgy

Liturgical prayer stands in contrast to personal prayer. If we wish to be precise, we should not say "liturgical prayer" but "the liturgical act". The roots of the liturgy lie, in fact, in the holy action; above all, in the Mass, which fulfils the command of the Lord given to the Apostles at the Last Supper: to comme-

morate him by doing the same as he had done. Its prayers have
their roots in this action; they express it and develop it. The
same is true of the sacraments. They, too, are in essence an act
which issues from God but which takes place through man and
in man. Their purpose is to catch hold of man in his actual world
and lead him to new life; and the words of the sacraments further this purpose. It is, however, in the so-called sacramentals
that the liturgical act reaches out most clearly beyond man into
the world. These are sacred customs and devotions which per-
vade our whole existence. Their core, too, is an action; it is upon
this that the prayer depends. Thus the participation of the faithful in the liturgical life must consist fundamentally in an action.
Unfortunately the opportunity for this has decreased, as time
has passed. There are two reasons for this – the increase in the
size of parishes and the fact that modern man has largely lost
the facility for symbolic action, because the intellectual and
ethical aspects of his religious life have been heavily stressed.
For this reason participation in the liturgical events today consists largely in the faithful's sharing in spirit in the actions of the
priest; for example, they learn not merely to pray "at" or "in"
the Holy Mass, but really to watch, to hear, to take part. It is
this which gives the prayers their true meaning.

Admittedly, there are parts of the liturgy which are based
entirely on prayer; for instance, the recital of Divine Office in
choir, which is done publicly in cathedrals and monastery churches. The individual priest says it privately in his breviary and
the various types of lay breviary indicate an attempt at participation on the part of the laity. But the public recital of the Divine Office is also connected with action, into which it is frequently transposed. The recital is carried out at definite places

34

inside the church; it is associated at certain climaxes with liturgical acts, such as the offering of incense; it is accompanied by
gestures: making the sign of the cross, bowing, genuflecting,
standing up, sitting down and rising, and so on.

Personal prayer is enacted entirely in the inner emotions of
the heart and in verbal expression; gesture and posture are
involved only by implication. The liturgy is in essence an action,
the enactment of which is a natural source of prayer. These,
then, are the two poles and the two main spheres of religious
life. They each proceed from their peculiar roots, have their own
special characteristics and their own irreplaceable significance.

In his personal prayer man is on his own, alone with God. The
liturgy, on the other hand, depends on the Christian community
as a whole. In it we speak not of "I" but of "we"; and this "we"
is very much more than a mere collection of individuals. In the
liturgy it is the Church, as a totality, which is speaking. Even
if several or many people separate themselves from her, she
continues to subsist, because she takes her origin not from the
individual's desire for community, but from the creative will
of God, who has taken humanity and united it with himself.
She was founded by Christ, born on the day of Pentecost and
has existed from then onwards, regardless of the wishes of individual men or individual ages. Made by Christ the bearer of
his message, she has authority over each and all: "If he will not
hear the Church, let him be to thee as the heathen and the
publican", the Lord said (Matt. 18:17). Indeed, she comprehends
not only the sum of humanity but, as Paul and John teach, the
sum of the world too. Thus, ultimately, the Church is the consecrated universe, the new and evolving creation under the rule
of the Holy Spirit (Eph. 1:3–23; Col. 1:13–20). Yet she does

not exist apart from the individual man. She exists in him. One and the same man is both a member of the Church, in so far as he is a part of her totality, and an individual, in so far as he is a personal soul which stands directly face to face with God.

It is this Church which acts and speaks in the liturgy. Thus the attitude of the individual when he co-operates in the liturgical action and says the liturgical prayer is different from his attitude in personal prayer. The two attitudes are not separate from one another, nor do they contradict one another; rather they represent essential opposite poles in the context of Christian existence. In this context a man ceases to be an isolated individual and becomes a member of the whole, a living organ through whom the great objective words and actions of the Church find expression.

Hence everything which may be termed 'law' takes on a new significance. Personal prayer, if it is to remain healthy and ordered, has need of laws; in other respects it should be dictated by what is personal and original in the emotions. In the sphere of liturgical prayer and action, however, such an originality would have no meaning and would simply turn into self-indulgence and disorder. In this sphere everything is governed by one sacred law. The present ordering of the liturgy is the fruit of the Church's long experience, the result of constant examination and re-shaping. This ordering is not only a counsel but also a standard, to which the individual must conform.

In the liturgy there is no freedom. Or, to be more accurate, there is no individual freedom. The freedom which is in the liturgy is exercised not by the will of the individual but by the will of the Church, governed by the Holy Spirit. This freedom finds its expression in broad slow movements which are worked out over the centuries and over the whole face of the earth. It finds its expression in the fact that the liturgy has no set goal, that it does not wish to "achieve" anything, but only to stand before God, to breathe and to develop, to love him and praise him. And it does all this according to an inner form which is the essence of the liturgy. Although this is freedom when looked at by itself, it becomes law for the individual.

Thus the liturgical act is a duty. The sacred actions have been fixed down to the smallest details by ancient tradition. The words have been examined by the Church and must be spoken as laid down by the liturgical books. The faithful, however, in co-celebrating the liturgy, will do so the more purely and correctly, the more sincerely they disregard their own private wishes. In personal prayer they may follow the impulses of their own heart; when they take part in the liturgy, they should entrust themselves to another impulse which has profounder and more powerful origins: the heart of the Church, whose heart-beat has continued down the centuries. Here their personal tastes, their individual desires and anxieties are alike irrelevant and must be left behind, so that each may enter into the great movement of the liturgical act. It is precisely through this abandoning of self that we can enjoy again and again the first fruits of liturgical worship: freedom and release from our daily concerns.

Popular Devotions

A study of liturgical and personal worship does not exhaust the whole of the religious life. A third type must now be considered. We may call this — although it is not an entirely satisfactory description — "popular devotions". To this category belong the

37

afternoon and evening devotions in the church, the family Rosary, the majority of popular religious customs, and so on.

This type of prayer cannot be defined in precise terms; perhaps it may best be said to lie between the liturgical and the personal but to be distinct from either. In contrast to personal prayer it has a communal character, for it is the needs not of the individual but of a larger group which find expression in it. Moreover, it is governed by tradition as well as by regulations and therefore has a certain authority as far as the individual is concerned. On the other hand it is much more private than the liturgy, for no particular devotions are in use throughout the whole Church, nor even throughout an entire country, but often are only found in certain dioceses. Sometimes there are even differences from parish to parish. Thus the passage of time and the particular conditions of a place, the variety of daily life and its changing conditions, are expressed in them much more directly than in the liturgy, which extends over a much wider area and in which the changes come much more slowly. Popular devotions are less strict in form than the liturgy. Their words are more informal and they indulge in greater detail. Imagination plays a far greater role. The tone is warmer and more direct. Because of this they lack the breadth of the liturgy, its austerity and power. They incline towards sentimentality and not infrequently fall a prey to random eccentricities.

Repetition is a favoured feature of popular devotions. "Never say the same thing twice" is a fundamental principle of liturgical prayer; in popular devotions, on the other hand, the same thing is said over and over again. They are the expression of a desire to linger in God's presence. Since, in a parish, the conditions are lacking for the saying of those prayers which make

38

up the liturgy, that is, for the recitation of the psalms, certain set prayers, such as the Our Father and Hail Mary are repeated in their place. So ordinary people find it easy to take part; on the other hand, there is a danger of monotony and lack of attention.

Since popular devotions are not necessarily offered by the Church as a whole, but by certain more limited parts of the whole, they produce a much stronger sense of community feeling. The Christian "we" is more vital in them than in the liturgy and hence the individual feels himself more deeply involved. The homeliness and intimacy which are felt in popular devotions come not only from the emotional character of the prayers and hymns, but also from this much closer community feeling of which they are the expression.

Reference might well be made here also to a particular aspect of popular devotions, that is, vernacular hymns. They are a direct expression of that depth of religious feeling from which popular devotions spring. Generally they do not have the strict form of liturgical hymns but are closer in style to the folk-song. In this way they carry over into the religious sphere the emotional depths of national feeling and the richness of popular imagination. Of course, they have their dangers too, for folk-songs thrive on sentimentality. Where the tradition of vernacular hymn-singing is not carefully preserved, the stricter hymns (both as regards content and form) fall easily into disuse and lighter, easily emotional hymns are preferred – not to mention some new hymns which are often simply inferior.

The Connection

These different spheres of the spiritual life are not simply parallel and unconnected but are related in a variety of ways. History shows how elements of one are constantly being absorbed into another. Several elements in the liturgy have originated in the personal life of some holy man or woman. And, similarly, the individual can enrich his devotional life by adapting the liturgical act in his own way and by making prayers from the Missal or Breviary part of his own spiritual life. Finally, as far as popular devotions are concerned, much of the liturgy was originally the expression of the spiritual life of a certain community and was later accorded general validity; in the same way, large parts of popular devotions – the hymns alone furnish ample proof of this – represent liturgical texts in freer form.

So far I have only spoken of historical links; the connections, however, go deeper. Liturgical and personal prayer are interdependent, each furthering the other. Each sphere has, indeed, its own roots and it is a good thing for each to grow purely from them; nonetheless they belong together and form the one unified Christian life.

In the liturgy the Church fulfils constantly the sacred functions originated by Christ himself and in this the individual is absorbed. He must, however, also lead his own personal spiritual life which comes from his own heart, if the liturgical act is not to become dead and superficial. It is true that it is the Church which is responsible for the sacred functions, but the Church becomes actual and real in the individual: in the faithful and in the priest. It is true that it is the act of the Church which carries out the liturgy, but this act passes through the souls of the individuals present. But if the individual has not learnt to face God, if his ear is not opened to hear nor his tongue loosened to speak, then the liturgical act does not pass through his living soul but only through his outer organs; and he who is listening, speaking and acting there, is no real person but an impersonal thing. In such a case the whole act loses its truth and its solemnity. Only when the individual prays as an individual too, can the great prayer of the Church come into the freedom and truth which is its own.

From the opposite point of view the individual needs the link with the prayer of the Church for his own personal prayer. And not only so that the prayer of the Church may support him and the intercession of the whole Church include him. In every living thing strength is, at the same time, weakness. Thus the solitude of inner confrontation, the freedom of emotion and the originality of its expression – everything, in fact, that constitutes the individuality of personal prayer – can become a danger. Solitude can turn to isolation, freedom to licence, originality to eccentricity. Its intimate nature needs broadening into objectivity and breadth. The liturgy is the "rule of prayer" not only in the sense that it tells the individual who enters its sphere how he must order his devotions, but also in the more profound sense that it contains permanent standards for the purity and soundness of all prayer. There is a great difference between "personal" prayer and "subjective" prayer. Prayer is personal when it springs from the dignity of a man admitting responsibility for himself, from the unique nature of the inner life, from the freedom of the child of God. It is subjective when the individual is seeking himself and substituting an assumed truthfulness for truth. There is the heresy of faith, when the

41

individual fashions the content of Revelation according to his personal experience and judgment. And there is, too, the heresy of prayer, when the individual relies on his own unpurified religious feelings and needs. The individual must go back again and again to the great pattern of the liturgy and must enact with it the greatness of its concepts and the clear symmetry of its actions; otherwise his personal prayer will drift into aloofness, sentimentality, eccentricity, and not infrequently even into abnormality and unhealthiness.

The same is true of popular devotions. Wherever liturgical life as such is not understood, loved and properly fostered, these devotions fall into a peculiar decline. The dangers of popular devotions are a lack of moderation, undisciplined invention, sugariness and a forced emotion. If popular devotions are left to the unpurified working of religious forces, aberrations are the result. There is, too, the danger of empty repetition no longer justified by content and of inner emptiness, when great thougths and genuine images are lacking. A parish which does not give to the liturgy the place which is its due, which lives off popular devotions and treats liturgical worship, in particular the Mass, as though it were popular devotions, must become spiritually impoverished. Faith and prayer lose their substance. Smallmindedness and narrowness are the result and an atmosphere in which only the old women feel themselves at home any longer. The step to loss of faith is no longer a big one.

In all this, however, the other side should not be forgotten. There is a type of liturgical endeavour which despises popular devotions and sees in them something inferior, superfluous and fundamentally harmful. It is this same mentality which prefers to see personal prayer, too, merely as an adaptation of the liturgical. This is both wrong and dangerous. Such behaviour resembles that of a person who says: "Humanity is enough for me: I do not need a people. The world is enough for me, I have no need of a country." Popular devotions express with regard to the religious life rather what is expressed by the connection between nation and family, country and parish, in the natural life. Everyone needs their depth, their warmth and their intimacy. An afternoon service which is conducted worthily and devoutly or an evening Rosary which is prayed as is right and proper are such beautiful things that anyone who rejects them condemns himself in so doing.

There is a lot which might be said in this vein; what has already been put forward is, however, enough for our purpose, which was to indicate very briefly the relationship between our personal prayer and the other prayers of the Church.

4

Eucharistic and Liturgical Piety

Theodor Schnitzler

There is an urgent necessity for giving thought to the question of eucharistic and liturgical piety and to education for this. The ideas of the Liturgical Revival are only just beginning to influence religious instruction. Not until immediately before and after the Second World War was our teaching on the Eucharist freed from an isolated devotion to the Blessed Sacrament, an isolated understanding of the Sacrifice of the Mass, and an isolated joy at Communion, and led towards a synthesis of the ideas about sacrifice and sacrificial meal, the sacrifice of Christ and the sacrifice of the Church, about Eucharist and Liturgy. It is distressing to note that almost our entire generation of adults, almost all the clergy, priests, religious and teachers were imbued with a eucharistic piety divorced from the liturgy. A German teacher, in his Catechism published in 1924 was able to introduce the section on the Mass in these words: "The question how the Christ Child comes into the tabernacle, why he is in fact there, leads us directly to the Holy Mass." He was referring to what the Mass meant not only to himself but to a large number of the faithful. Eucharistic piety, then, faces what are clearly incalculable pedagogic problems. It is a question not only of education but also of a very necessary re-education.

If we wish to consider the eucharistic devotion which is our educational aim, we have to ask ourselves first of all what devotion is. Thus we establish from the beginning that devotion is a response to dogma. Just as the responsory follows a reading, the divine word of the reading being re-coined as praise and thanksgiving to God in the responsory, so devotion is the response of the person at prayer to the Revelation; devotion meets the divine word of doctrinal theology with praise and thanks and petition. Devotion is addressed to "you", whereas doctrine refers to "he". From this it inevitably follows that devotion can never be undogmatic. Nor should it take as its starting-point a dogma that is narrow and confined. Rather must it, on principle, take its direction from all the rich fullness of faith. Devotion which tried to orientate itself entirely according to individual points of dogma would soon fall into error, as history has proved often enough. An example of this is the devotion to Christ which either emphasizes one-sidedly his divinity without his humanity or else his humanity without his divinity.

Our subject, however, is not simply devotion in general but eucharistic piety or devotion. The most holy sacrament of the Eucharist is both object and source of this devotion. Through the divine power at work in it, the Eucharist fosters and encourages devotion in four ways: it fosters the prayerful life of faith, the efficacy of our witness, the "pietas" between God and man, our inwardness and fervour. Likewise faith, witness, love, and fervour should be the adornments of the individual approaching the Eucharist.

When speaking of the Eucharist we should keep two aspects of it in mind: the Eucharist as the fact of Christ's sacrifice and also the Eucharist as a ceremony, as a liturgy, as a harmony of prayers, hymns, signs and actions of the Church, which all clothe this mystery. In the first instance devotion is primarily centred upon dogma, in the second primarily upon the liturgy. Leaving the treatment of eucharistic devotion in the sphere of dogma to books on doctrine, we should like to confine our attention to the liturgical sphere. Our claim is that the celebration of the Eucharist, which is the liturgy, is in Pius XII's great words: *"fons et centrum totius pietatis"*.

Let us begin with the last of the four effects of the Eucharist mentioned above. The liturgy is a means of devout fervour.

Here a question, almost a protest, forces itself upon us. Is it not precisely this fervour which we miss in the Roman liturgy? We have only to think of the austere, cool quality of the Canon of the Mass or of the basilical, marble solemnity of a Preface. In fact, it is true of the Mass not only that "all its beauty is from within" but also that its fervour, too, is from within. We must learn to see behind the texts the images of which there is often only a hint. Let us take as an example the opening rites of the Mass. The psalm said at the foot of the altar was once used as an Easter hymn in the procession to the altar after baptism and is permeated with the radiant picture of the Risen One. It is on seeing this picture that we call the Lord: My joy! The *Introit,* the opening hymn, would have us see that Christ the Shepherd, the King of his people, leads his own, the chosen people, the sheep of his herd, into his Father's house to sing his praises, to celebrate the sacrifice, to share in the abundant meal of grace. Therefore the Introit tries to evoke in the fervour of every supplicant the invocation: Lord, you are my Shepherd and my King, you are our Mediator and Redeemer and our Advocate with the Father. Then, even more so, the *Kyrie* guides us to

46

this deepening of our fervour. For with each cry it is sounding a different tune, one which has been borrowed from the hymns of the earliest ages. At one moment it glorifies the Lord as Greek paganism praised the sun: *Kyrie* – Sun of our existence! At the next the same greeting is dedicated to him as was once used for the kings and emperors of the Greek era: *Kyrie* – the Emperor of the new Kingdom of God, King of my heart! Next homage is paid him with the invocation reserved by the Jews for the One Lord, the great God: *Kyrie* – you omnipresent God! In the *Gloria* these words of awe and heartfelt love are the dominant feature of the text, as we can see when we unravel the verse-form of the hymn and consider the individual shouts of joy: Lord! God! Heavenly King! Almighty! Son! Only-Begotten! Lamb! The Collect is the solemn invocation which the High Priest Jesus Christ addresses to the Father for his people, in which he uplifts and outstretches his wounded hands, as when he hung on the Cross and as the epistle to the Hebrews saw him: and in it the liturgy offers again the means by which we can gain the fervour of a vision which can soon be transformed into inward prayer: You, our High Priest – our Mediator and Redeemer – you who show your pierced hands to the Father, speak to the Father for us. Any devotional instruction must take care to see that we do not only take part in the formal acts and words but at the same time make the background of ideas and images our own. Then both aims are fulfilled: on the one hand the liturgical act is flooded with personal warmth, on the other hand the blood transfusion for this warmth springs from the liturgy itself.

The liturgy is not always cold; sometimes it soars above its restraint. In the well-known words of Guardini, which he adap-

47

ted from Nietzsche, the liturgy is like a volcano covered with glaciers; so closely are cold and fire united in it. As on such a mountain-top, so too in the liturgy there sometimes breaks forth over the glaciers an eruption of inner fire. We can see this happening in two examples. The Canon begs for the transubstantiation in ponderous, dispassionate terms which stem from the language of law: "This our offering, do thou, O God, vouchsafe in all things to bless, consecrate, approve, make reasonable and acceptable: that it may become for us the body and blood", and now a priceless flower blossoms from the rock-like text: "of thy most beloved Son, our Lord Jesus Christ." Here the words of explanation *(Filius dilectus)* are brought to a climax in the superlative: *"Dilectissimi filii tui Domini nostri Jesu Christi!"* Whoever prays these significant and meaningful words and takes them to heart, learns to affirm them: "Indeed you are the dearly-beloved, the sole beloved of my life!" The other example is the tiny half-sentence from the prayer of preparation for Communion: ". . . never suffer me to be separated from thee." There the same note sounds as in the *"Anima Christi":* "O never part from me!" There the cry of St. Paul becomes a prayer: "Who then shall separate us from the love of Christ? Shall tribulation? Or distress? Or famine? Or nakedness? Or danger? Or persecution? Or the sword? But in all these things we overcome because of him that hath loved us; for I am sure that neither death nor life nor any other creature can separate us from the love of God which is in Christ Jesus our Lord." Step by step we find similar hidden flowers of fervour in the holy Mass, which we must recognize and gather up. Then the celebration of the Mass will indeed become a *"fons pietatis"*.

It is only possible to discover such fervour in the liturgical texts, when we go to Mass with a willingness to do so. It is impossible to draw water from a well unless a suitable vessel is prepared beforehand to be let down into the depths. This willingness, this preliminary fervour, from which we can gain the fervour of the liturgy itself, has its opportunity in the time for preparation and meditation, in the homily and words of commentary. Here then, too, there is the possibility of a development in the instruction given on the Eucharist.

If we now consider the aspect of *"pietas"*, we will realize once again that the liturgy is our source. In innumerable texts it tells us of God's fatherly love which gives us his only-begotten Son and "with him all". At the same time the general attitude underlying all the texts and rites is that of *"pietas"* as the filial love, which, led by Christ our brother, we feel for the Father. This love is expressed in the reverential kissing of the altar, in the lifting up of the eyes and the folding of the hands (which shows their desire to lie between the hands of God as in the medieval feudal oath), in the measured bows, in the rising up of the incense. In short, all the performance of these sacred signs is, as it were, a school of reverential devotion to God. The same is true of the liturgical texts. Only it is again a prerequisite that we allow ourselves to be both moved and moulded by this school. We must fulfil the intention of the liturgy: *facere quod facit ecclesia* – and not act according to our own selfish and rebellious instincts. To do this we need to be both thoughtful and attentive. The celebrating priest should not carry out the ceremonies or speak the words mechanically and the congregation should not merely sit through it without watching, without inwardly offering the sacrifice with the priest. To do this we need a time for meditation beforehand to render us alert and receptive, so that the sacred act can make its efficacy fully felt. For the liturgy to be our school of reverence, of pietas, of filial love, we must go to this school by the road of reverential and devout preparation.

We turn now to the aspect of efficacy and usefulness which lies in devotion. The bishop says to the candidates for ordination: "Know what you fulfil, imitate what you do, so that in celebrating the mystery of the death of the Lord you may provide for the mortification of your members from all vices and passions." Here we find an ideal summary of all Christian asceticism. Sacrifice is the summit of human development, because it unites us with the Head, Christ. "To suffer with Christ on the cross" is held as an ideal of life before every Christian. It is with our sacrificing and crucified Head that we reach the hands of the Father, our final goal and end. This basic conception of the liturgy is given expression in many different words: *"Nosmetipsos tibi perfice munus aeternum!"* or *"In quo omnis sanctitatis fontem constituisti!"* or *"Ex quo martyrium omne sumpsit exordium!"* It is expressed daily in the repeated offertory word *"Suscipere"* in the prayers of oblation. In "Receive, holy Father", "Receive, O holy Trinity", "May we be received by thee", "May the Lord receive the sacrifice" are echoed the *"Suscipe"* of the martyred Stephen and the prayer of consecration in the Spiritual Exercises of St. Ignatius. Whoever truly prays and offers with the priest at Holy Mass is being formed into the greatest possible efficacy for God, to sacrifice. But here, too, it is necessary once again for us to go to this school of sacrifice, so that, as the ordination admonition demands, we "realize what we are doing".

50

We should like to show this efficacy by one other example, although, in fact, a whole Christian moral philosophy might be discussed here. We mean the basic disposition of gladness of heart. The first words on the threshold of the altar run: "To God, who giveth joy to my youth." The last words on leaving the altar are: "*Deo gratias.*" At the opening of the Canon come the words: "Let us give thanks!" At the end of the Communion we take the chalice with the words, "With gladness and joy I call upon the Lord". It is not only the Preface for Pentecost which speaks of "overflowing joy", but every *Gloria,* every final doxology of the Canon, the numerous Offertories which accompany the offering of the gifts with the melody of joy, because "God loves a cheerful giver". The entire Mass is turned into a symphony of joy. We may and must let ourselves be carried away by it, if we are to discover the basic disposition of the early Christian community, who took the Eucharistic Bread "*in exsultatione cordis*". If, however, we join in, if we let ourselves be infected by this joy, we will gain one of the most important dispositions for all Christian efficacy. For gladness of heart is the enemy, and the most victorious one, of egotism, of our inability to love. It opens the way to all fervour and zeal for Christian endeavour.

We come now to the fundamental aspect of eucharistic and liturgical devotion, the realization of the life of faith. What is expressed by catechism and doctrinal theology in theses, dogmas and propositions, is celebrated in the liturgy. The liturgy celebrates it in loving commemoration, makes it actual and efficacious. In doing so, the liturgy creates the possibility in which the "he" of theology is transformed into the "you" of prayer, of thanksgiving, of real encounter. All the riches of faith are drawn, too, into this liturgical celebration, not just in the feasts of the Church's year, not just in the daily readings and pericopes, not just in so many antiphons, but rather the liturgy is directed and permeated throughout by the life of faith. It fulfils the fundamental law referred to by Pius XII in *Mediator Dei,* when he translated the well-known axiom *"lex orandi lex credendi"* more meaningfully as: "May the law of faith be the basis for the law of prayer." In this way living and praying with the liturgy leads us to the true life of faith. We must, then, open our minds without any exclusiveness or narrowness to all the wealth of the liturgy and all the riches of the professions of faith in it. We must know the catechism so well that we can find it again in the Missal and make it the content of our prayer. Guided by Revelation, we find in the liturgy the summary of the revelation of faith. What St. Ambrose said of the liturgical psalms is true of the liturgy: "Here Jesus is not only born but also accepts the redeeming Passion of his Body and gives himself up to death, rises again, sits on the right hand of the Father . . . Here is the sublime confession of faith."

In brief, we may affirm that the fourfold effect of devotion (faith expressed in prayer, filial love of God, efficacy and fervour) is taught, moulded, and set aflame by the liturgy. To achieve this, preparation and meditation and the receptivity which result from them are prerequisites. Equally relevant is the perseverance in these dispositions outside the liturgy in the struggle and everyday life of Christian witness. In this way eucharistic devotion becomes a fountain springing from the waters of the Redeemer, moistening and fertilizing the arid land all around and falling back into its well only to spring forth again with new strength.

52

5
Psalmodic Piety

JOSEF PASCHER

THE importance of psalm-singing in the Church rests basically on the fact that the present Book of Psalms belongs to the precious treasure of inspired books. No-one doubts that these hymns were given to us by God, so that we might pray them, just as we pray the prayer which the Lord gave to his apostles with the words "Thus therefore shall you pray: Our Father . . ." As far as the psalms are concerned, it is certainly not accidental that they have been handed down to us as songs, for variety and adaptability as regards performance are essentially part of their character. Devotion to the psalms, that is the use of the psalms in our spiritual life, has always had as its basis the spontaneous response of the individual soul and has never demanded any accurate reconstruction of the original situation in the sacred texts. This does not affect the indubitable fact that a deep textual study of the psalms and an understanding of the literal meaning is a healthy initial basis for the singing of these hymns. In spite of the freedom of individual response, the use of the psalms remains, nonetheless, within certain limits, set by the devotion of the Old and (as far as the Church today is concerned) of the New Testament. In view of this, there are basically two ways in which they can be used: completely freely by the individual or liturgically.

1. The Spontaneous Use by the Individual

The Book of Psalms presents the broad picture of man praying and singing before God in all the stages from deepest sorrow to highest bliss, at all the levels of human inter-relationship, in happiness and misery, in guilt and holiness, in love and hate. Since these songs stem from the East of the last thousand years before Christ and from a pre-Christian Jewish piety, there may well be some expressions or floods of feeling which will seem incomprehensible or antipathetic to the twentieth century Western Christian; yet the wealth of thought and feeling which he will find in them and his freedom of response make these inspired songs both sublime and practicable for use in Christian prayer today.

Christian devotion constantly finds itself and its intentions reflected in the psalter. Often a word from the psalms touches the human heart like a revelation, opens it and sends it on its flight towards God, borne up by the Spirit which filled the holy singer so long ago. Time and again, through the grace of the same Spirit, comfort and joy, courage and strength and gladness stream forth as God's answer into the human soul.

It is true that it is only to a limited extent that the book of Psalms provides prayers for definite clearly defined intentions, as some prayer-books do in order to supply the faithful with a formula for prayer in all life's situations. Nonetheless there are psalms for times of affliction or of repentance, psalms in praise of God, psalms for morning and evening, etc. But it is the very character of the psalms which explains the Church's age-old procedure of having the psalms recited simply in numerical order. She leaves to chance how the psalm strikes the individual praying it. It is as if she wanted to achieve this moment of surprise, the kindling from above of the Spirit, who "bloweth where he listeth". Except, then, for the relatively few cases of psalms which are directly applicable to particular circumstances, the *lectio continua* is probably the right method for the private prayer of the individual too. Then the word of the psalm will touch the individual the more closely and frequently, the more he realizes his position, bound down right and left, in the midst of the grief and joy in the world around him. If he is happy himself, he will, when he prays the psalms, share the sorrows of his fellow-men, both near and far, and take upon himself the cry of distress to God on other's behalf. Even if he himself is in God's love through penance and grace, he will bow under his brother's burden of sins to beg for him and with him. "If thou, O Lord, wilt mark iniquities: Lord, who shall stand it?"

In one country the Christian devotes himself to his faith and religion in undisturbed freedom, offers his Masses on feast-days and Sundays in peace and quiet, while in another place a hot or cold war is being waged against the Church. In the psalm the individual will come across the cry of the persecuted for help as "the waters rise about his throat" and once again the distress of others will be mirrored in his soul and the psalm will be the prayer of brotherly love, as much as if he himself were being hounded by "wild dogs" . . .

It was of great importance for the history of the psalms in the Church that people learnt to understand and pray them from the New Testament point of view, that is, mainly christologically. For this guidance was found to a certain extent in Holy Scripture. The Lord himself had interpreted Ps. 109 messianically in the dispute with the Jews (Mk 12:35 ff.). Peter did

55

similarly in the speech at Pentecost (Acts 2:34f.) with the same
psalm and with Psalm 15 (3:25–28). The same thing happened
with Ps. 2 in the prayer of the afflicted community (4:25f.) and
in Paul's sermon in Antioch of Pisidia (13:33). There the Apostle
explained Ps. 15:10 also in terms of the Resurrection of Christ.
The christological view of the psalms is developed most strongly
in the Epistle to the Hebrews.

The Commentaries of the Fathers made use of the christological principle to a very great extent. The utterances in the psalms
centre around Christ, whether they are Vox Patris ad Christum,
Christi ad Patrem, Ecclesiae ad Christum, Christi ad Ecclesiam,
etc. The application of this principle effected a real increase in
devotion to the psalms and it would be true to say that even
today it rules the use of the psalms in prayer in the Catholic
Church, especially in the liturgy.

The christological principle is, at root, simply a conclusion
drawn from the song-like character of the psalms. When
Augustine constantly hears the voice of Christ or of the Church
in his Commentary on the Psalms, he is hearing the response
of his own heart to the words of the psalm. It is here, too, that
the real justification of this procedure lies and it should emphatically not be confused with a biblical exegesis in the modern
sense.

It must, however, be pointed out that the recognition of this
fact has one inevitable consequence as far as the dogmatic
usefulness of the commentaries of the Fathers is concerned. The
commentary cannot be used without examination to support
what is, in fact, an exegetical statement. Whether and how far
this is possible, is something to be examined separately in each
case. To put it another way: the commentary gives more indica-

tion of the commentator's response, or of the commentator himself, or of his theology (which determines his response), than of the right interpretation of the psalms themselves.

It is only on the principle of an individual response that particular features of the psalms can be accepted by the modern Christian. For only in that way can allowance be made for the individuality of every era. A problem which is today once again the subject of lively discussion is that posed by the imprecatory psalms. It is certainly no bad sign for the piety of the New Testament that it revolts at the thought of cursing its enemies and that the degree of severity of a curse does not come into question.

When the Church recommends the psalms to the faithful and enjoins the reading of the Book of Psalms in its entirety upon her priests, she cannot wish that the enemies of God or the Church should be cursed. (For this is not the meaning even of excommunication.) The Church must, then, see the possibility of singing the imprecatory psalm without cursing. The text of the imprecatory psalm is read, let us say, by a man informed by the New Testament, who might perhaps by nature and temperament be capable of cursing, but who knows and affirms in his inmost soul the Sermon on the Mount and the prayer of the Crucified Lord for his enemies. What response does the imprecation awaken in the Christian's heart? It is very possibly a simple dismissal: Words like these are not prayers! Texts like these ought to be removed from the Breviary! But then he begins to reflect: Is it not the intention of the divine Spirit that inspired these texts, that we should hear behind these curses the sentences of condemnation in the judgment which is to come? After all, the Lord himself spoke of the "weeping

57

and gnashing of teeth" of the damned. Indeed he will himself speak sentences of damnation at the last day – in a New Testament sense, of course. The response of the Christian heart must be: When you sing these words, you are perhaps calling judgment down on your own heart; as he who bears hatred does when he prays: "Forgive us our trespasses, as we forgive them, that trespass against us."

The principle of individual response follows from the poetic, musical character of the texts. If one starts from the music without the words it is clear, without more ado, that an exact exegesis is impossible, even though the freedom of response is not absolute and unrestricted. The combination of words and music in the song increases the restrictions. Yet there still remains a great deal of latitude. There is also the possibility of applying yet further restrictions if the psalm is used for a particular occasion and spontaneous response limited by the more definite intention. This can be the case in private singing. It is to a great extent the system in liturgical usage.

2. Psalms in the Liturgy

The Canonical Hours consist in the main of the singing of the psalms. The reading takes second place and is far less extensive. The performance of the psalmody follows the principles which generally hold good for the singing of the psalms – principles which have been developed above.

In general, the psalms were recited in the order of the psalter even before the days of St. Benedict and for this purpose they were divided between the Vigils (today called Matins) and

Vespers. Psalms 1–108 were very early allotted to Matins and those from 109 onwards to Vespers throughout the seven-day week. For the early prayer of Matins (today called Lauds) suitable psalms were selected from the whole sequence. The same thing was done for the Little Hours. For the psalmody of Matins and Vespers of the week (Sunday to Saturday) therefore, only the principle of individual response can be valid. Admittedly one will have to favour the Early Fathers' method – with its christological interpretation of the psalms as a certain limitation of the response, though without any constraint on the free movement of the Spirit.

On the other hand, where the choice of psalms has been governed by clearly determinable motives as at Lauds, anyone saying the Breviary will have to be guided by the basic idea behind the choice. Certain observations, which are important for psalmodic devotion of the person using the Breviary, may be made concerning this choice and the principles by which it is usually governed. Basically two possibilities can be distinguished. There is the rare case when the psalm is useful as a whole for a definite occasion. In the majority of cases it is a verse or a section of the psalm which makes it appear suitable for an actual occasion. Examples of both possibilities can be given from Lauds. For an Hour which is so clearly one of praise, the *Laudate* psalms were an obvious choice and for this reason Psalms 148–150 have from the earliest times formed part of Lauds. On the other hand, Ps. 62 has to thank its position in the same Hour to the verse: "*Deus, Deus meus, ad te de luce vigilo*" (O God, thou art my God; to thee at dawn I keep vigil), in which the fact that the prayer is being said in the early morning before sunrise is beautifully expressed. The verse does not stand alone, but is followed by lines of longing for God, which express with extraordinary effectiveness the singer desires God, although the image is different from that of dawn and the approaching sun. The first verse, as we know, is a translation error from the Septuagint version and is today, according to the *Hebraica veritas* (the Latin text of the Pontifical Biblical Institute) superseded by the words: *"Deus, Deus meus es, sollicite te quaero."* (O God, thou art my God; how eager my quest for thee.)

The principle of choosing appropriate psalms, which is relatively rarely heeded in the weekday psalter, is the dominant one on feast-days. Historically, though, a different principle seems to have been obtained here too, in the first instance. At Easter, as well as on all the feasts of martyrs, the Sunday psalms were taken over, clearly because it was desired to make a day into a feast by putting it on a par with Sunday.

Whether the formation of special series for feasts is anterior to the weekday psalter and the Office of Martyrs must remain undecided. The well-known psalter for the Vigil of Christmas must, at any rate, go back to the fifth century and possibly even further. On it depend the psalter for feasts of the Blessed Virgin and of holy Virgins. Therefore it follows that it is just this group which is particularly illuminating as regards the method of singing the psalms desired by the Church.

The series for Christmas contains the following nine psalms and antiphons:

2 *Dominus dixit ad me: Filius meus es tu, ego hodie genui te.* (The Lord told me: Thou art my Son, I have begotten thee this day.)

18 *Tamquam sponsus Dominus procedens de thalamo suo.* (The Lord comes as a bridegroom from his bed.)

44 *Diffusa est gratia in labiis tuis, propterea benedixit te Deus in aeternum.* (Thy lips overflow with gracious utterance; the blessings God has granted thee can never fail.)

47 *Suscepimus, Deus, misericordiam tuam in medio templi tui.* (Sheltered in thy temple, God, we sought and found deliverance.)

71 *Orietur in diebus Domini abundantia pacis, et dominabitur.* (Justice in his days shall thrive, and the blessings of peace.)

84 *Veritas de terra orta est, et iustitia de caelo prospexit.* (Faithfulness grows up out of the earth, and from heaven, justice looks down.)

88 *Ipse invocavit me, alleluia: Pater meus es tu, alleluia.* (Thou art my Father, he will cry out to me, alleluia.)

95 *Laetentur caeli, et exsultet terra ante faciem Domini, quoniam venit.* (Rejoice, heaven, and let earth be glad before the face of the Lord because he comes.)

97 *Notum fecit Dominus, alleluia, salutare suum, alleluia.* (The Lord has given proof of his saving power.)

Each of the nine psalms is provided with an antiphonal verse. This antiphon is, in each case, taken from the psalm itself and it is not difficult to see that the verses are chosen because they can be interpreted to refer to Christmas. Thus the principle of their selection is recognizable. In a few cases the whole psalm is interpreted with reference to Christmas. This is true, for example, of Ps. 44, the theme of which is the marriage of the King's Son. It is clear that in it there is a mystical interpretation of the mystery of the Incarnation. The Son of God is the bridegroom and

61

human nature his bride. The antiphon celebrates the beauty of the young king. Perhaps the compiler of the Christmas psalter saw other psalms too, in their entirety, as sustaining a Christmas interpretation. The Incarnation could be understood as God's answer to the plotting of the adversary. One can scarcely go far wrong in interpreting Ps. 18, if one thinks of Christ as the "Sun of Righteousness". Moreover, the Latin translation, which the liturgist had in front of him, has changed the reading: "He has made the sun into his throne" and altered the image to: "He hath set his tabernacle in the sun." This tabernacle is then the chamber: "and he, as a bridegroom coming out of his bride-chamber." This text may have been chosen in view of his having been born of Mary.

In striking contrast to such Christmas imagery is Ps. 47 and its antiphon. With an appropriate antiphon many other psalms would equally well suit the feast on which we received God's mercy. Perhaps its choice was due to the words "in the midst of thy temple" and the motif of the mountain which is particularly stressed in the text of the psalm. Probably the Christmas Office, like the old formularies for the feasts of saints, was compiled for a definite place of worship. Already in the fourth century, at the time when Liberius was building his basilica on the Esquiline hill, Rome had established the shrine "the Lord's crib" to honour our Lord's Nativity. If the psalms were compiled specially for the Liberian basilica, Ps. 47 supports an unusually clear interpretation. The Esquiline hill is the mountain and the basilica on its ridge the temple in whose midst we "have received thy mercy".

The motif of the mountain plays a part at the Station at St. Mary Major too. It is well-known that for certain Wednesdays the Roman lectionary lists not one but two readings for the great basilica of Our Lady on the Esquiline. The first of them is on Ember Wednesday in Advent: "In the last days the mountain of the house of the Lord shall be prepared on the top of mountains, and it shall be exalted above the hills, and all nations shall flow unto it. And many people shall go, and say: Come and let us go up to the mountain of the Lord, and to the house of the God of Jacob" (Isai. 2:2f.). On Ember Wednesday in Lent the pericope of the giving of the Law on Mount Sinai is read (Ex. 24:12-18), while on the Wednesday of the autumn Ember Days the words of the reading from Amos ring out: "And the mountains shall drop sweetness and every hill shall be tilled" (Amos 9:13). Even though the choice was probably made because of the connection with the harvest, nonetheless the image of the mountain must have been instrumental too. The choosing of the daily texts according to such local factors is no rarity in the Missal, as H. Grisar[1] has shown.

Psalm 71 also belongs to the psalms the reasons for the choice of which are quite clear. The christological and Christmas reference was found by the old liturgists in the first verse: *"Deus, iudicium tuum regi da et iustitiam tuam filio regis."* (Grant to the king, O God, thy own skill in judgment; the inheritor of a throne, may he be just, as thou art just.) Yet this sentence is not taken as the antiphon, but the verse *"Orietur in diebus"* (In his days shall thrive) – in itself less meaningful. It looks almost as though the choice had been decided by the verse which immediately precedes it and which alludes to the miracle with Gedeon's fleece (Judges 6:37f.): *"Descendet sicut pluvia in vellus."*

---

[1] *Das Missale im Lichte der römischen Stadtgeschichte (Freiburg, 1925).*

(Let the dew fall on the fleece.) The whole psalm gives rise so vividly to thoughts of the coming King of Peace that the choice is entirely understandable.

Ps. 84 owes its place in the Christmas Vigil to the verse: "Faithfulness grows up out of the earth: and from heaven justice looks down" (v. 12). Clearly the liturgy sees in this text an expression of the Incarnation and for this reason chooses it as antiphon. If, however, one examines the whole psalm, the preceding verse must certainly be taken into account once again: "Mercy and faithfulness meet in one; how justice and peace are united in one embrace!" (v. 11). But elsewhere, too, the psalm has sentences which can easily be taken as references to the advent of the Redeemer, as, for instance, the opening words: "What blessing thou hast granted to this land of thine, restoring Jacob from captivity, pardoning thy people's guilt, burying away the record of their sins."

The reason for the choice of Ps. 88 is quite plainly seen from the antiphon: "Thou art my father, alleluia, he will cry out to me" (v. 27). It is equally certain that the following verse, too, played a part in its choice: "And I will acknowledge him as my firstborn, overlord to all the kings of earth" (v. 28). This central group of verses is again not isolated, but everything which by its noble promise points to the ideal king is taken by the Christmas liturgy as a reference, to the new-born Redeemer.

The psalms 95 and 97 close the Christmas psalter. It is striking, when one reviews the series for feasts, how frequently the group of psalms 95 – 98 are given preference. An ingenious hypothesis maintains that they replace other psalms, which are today sung at Vespers, and belong to the Vesper series 109 – 150. At Christmas, then, psalms 95 and 97 must have been substitutes for psalms 129 and 131, when the observance of the rule (originally only binding for the weekday psalter) that the Vigil should take its psalms from the series 1 – 108 and Vespers from 109 –150 was required on feast-days too.

If the hypothesis holds good as far as Christmas is concerned, then the choice of psalms 95 and 97 is, in any case, exceptionally appropriate. Yet the choice is still completely intelligible without the hypothesis. The choice of two '*Cantate*' psalms for Christmas is an especially obvious one in view of the '*Gloria*' sung by the angels. Moreover, both psalms contain the motif of the coming, of the fulfilment of our waiting, which has dominated the liturgy of the Advent season and been the atmosphere underlying it.

In Ps. 95 the antiphon presents just this thought as the emphasis for the whole song: "Rejoice, heaven, and let earth be glad before the face of the Lord: because he cometh" (v. 11a 13a). Ps. 97 has an antiphon which is in excellent keeping with the Christmas mystery: "The Lord has given proof, alleluia, of his saving power, alleluia" (v. 2a).

In Ps. 95 the verse: "Bring sacrifice, come into his courts: worship the Lord in his holy temple" (v. 8b 9a) deserves special attention. Perhaps, as was suggested in the case of Ps. 47, the text has been taken by the liturgist as a reference to the Liberian basilica. In fact, psalms 95, 11 and 13 were used in St. Mary Major ad praesepe as the Offertory of the first Mass of Christmas.

"No corner of the world but has witnessed how our God can save" (v. 3) in psalm 97 was definitely given a Christmas interpretation. The Roman antiphonary uses the text in the Gradual and Communion of the third Christmas Mass and originally used the whole psalms in the Introit.

Very probably the Christmas psalter was compiled for the shrine ad praesepe Domini on the Esquiline hill. In spite of that, this series of nine psalms was again adapted in that very place and the group of psalms which we sing today on the feast of the Circumcision, on the 1st January, was formed.

We know that this group was used in the Christmas matins at St. Mary Major. It can be further shown that originally the series was different (cp. MThZ. 8, 1957, p. 199f.):

2 18 23 44 47 71 84 86 95

It was increased by the Benedictines to twelve:

2 18 23 44 47 71 84 86 95 96 97 98

From there it was reduced by three numbers to the present Roman order:

2 18 23 44   86 95 96 97 98

A comparison of the old series with the series for Christmas gives an interesting insight into the devotion to the psalms of the makers of the liturgy.

At the Circumcision only Ps. 23 and Ps. 86 are new, replacing Ps. 88 and Ps. 97. It is quite clear why Ps. 86 was substituted for Ps. 88. The antiphon shows the reason for the choice of Ps. 86: *"Homo natus est in ea et ipse fundavit eam Altissimus"* (Man was born in her, she was founded by no other than the Most High.) (v. 5). Originally a reference to the Holy City, the verse is interpreted as referring to Mary, the Mother of God. Thus while Ps. 88 glorifies the fatherhood of God, Ps. 86 sings of the motherhood of Mary, and this in a church which had been dedicated by Pope Sixtus III to the Theotokos, the Mother of

God, after the Council of Ephesus shortly before (in 431) had raised the title Mother of God to a dogma. The Marian interpretation in the old Roman psalter was even more striking. The antiphon verse runs: *"Mater Sion dicit homo et homo factus est in ea, et ipse fundavit eam Altissimus"* (ed. Weber, p. 214).

The introduction of Ps. 23 is accounted for by the antiphon verse: *"Elevamini, portae aeternales, et introibit Rex Gloriae"* (Swing back, immemorial gates and let the King enter in triumph.) (v. 7). Here, too, the Marian idea must have influenced the choice, since the motif of the gate has at all times been a popular one in devotion to Mary. It should also be borne in mind that the motif of the mountain, too, influences its choice: "Who dares climb the mountain of the Lord, and appear in his sanctuary?" (v. 3). It is possible that v. 7 was thought of as a reference to the doors of the basilica. Psalm 23 is also used in the Missal on the Ember Wednesday of Advent (Gradual 7) and at the Vigil of Christmas (Introit, Offertory, Communion), both times at St. Mary Major.

If the connection between the psalters of Christmas and the Circumcision of the Lord is illuminating as far as the motives for choosing the different psalms are concerned and thus beneficial for devotion to the psalms, the same thing is true of the change to the series for the Blessed Virgin Mary and for the Virgins. At St. Mary Major the series for Christmas has probably been reformed for the Theotokos in the form for feasts of the Blessed Virgin, which was influenced by the Benedictine psalter.

Circumcision: 2 18 23 44   86 95 96 97 98

B. V. M.   8 18 23 44 45 86 95 96 97

Ps. 2 has been substituted for Ps. 8 and Ps. 98 for Ps. 45. Only in the cases of Ps. 44 and Ps. 45 are the antiphons still taken from the psalm. Since it is taken from a psalm recited in its entirety, v. 5 of Psalm 44 should be seen as referring to the royal Bridegroom, even when it is an antiphon, and not imputed to the Bride, as often happens to v. 8 in translations of liturgical texts. Yet there is an unmistakable change. At Christmas and the Circumcision the Bride is scarcely Mary. On the Office of the Blessed Virgin, however, it is right that we should think of her.

In the form of the old Roman psalter (ed. Weber p. 102) v. 6 is the antiphon to Ps. 45, only with the halves of the verse changed round: "God helps it with his countenance. God dwells within her, and she stands unmoved." Probably v. 5 can be included too: "But the city of God, enriched with deeply flowing rivers, is the chosen sanctuary of the most High." "Deeply flowing rivers" was already interpreted as the Holy Ghost by Augustine: "Clearly that stream of the river is to be understood as the Holy Ghost, through which every pious soul that believes in Christ is sanctified" (Enarr. m. Ps. 45, n. 8; CChr. 38, 5 23). For the old liturgist *"Deus in medio eius"* (God dwells within her) in the connection with the stream from the Spirit pointed so clearly to the conception by the Holy Ghost that he put Ps. 45 into the Psalter of the Blessed Virgin and sacrificed Ps. 98.

Besides this Ps. 2 was replaced by Ps. 8. It is understandable that the powerfully Messianic Ps. 2 was always retained at Christmas even in St. Mary Major, since the series for the Circumcision still refers to the Incarnation, even though in accordance with the council of Ephesus, in a Marian sense. Now, however, it is a matter of arranging a feast of the Blessed Virgin and the liturgist is attracted by Ps. 8. Exactly what turned his attention to this psalm in particular is not entirely clear. Probably v. 6 provided the reason: "Thou hast placed him only a little below the angels." Then, too, the psalm is one which praises virginity, which, according to earlier piety, is an angelic virtue. Besides this Marian motive, there is another possibility. Ps. 2 was chosen in praise of the Son of God. Ps. 8 could be sung to the Son of Mary: "Thou hast made the lips of children, of infants at the breasts, vocal with praise" (v. 3) points to the mother with the Child. In fact a familiar Nativity tableau is revealed to us in the verses: "Thou hast placed him only a little below the angels, crowning him with glory and honour, and bidding him rule over the works of thy hands. Thou hast put them all under his dominion, the sheep and the cattle, and the wild beasts besides the birds in the sky, and the fish in the sea that travel by the sea's paths" (v. 6–9). It is an old tradition to portray the Divine Child with ox and ass. A fourth century representation in the catacomb of St. Sebastian (DACL 1 2056; innumerable further examples here) shows that in the Nativity shrine in the Eternal City there was certainly a picture in which the animals were to be seen and that in this way, too, there might have been a reason for the choice of Ps. 8. Leclercq, probably on good authority, maintains that a Nativity tableau was to be seen in the grotto ad praesepe Domini (DACL III 3026 f.). The representation of the Birth of Christ with ox and ass goes back to Isa. 1:3: "Ox recognizes its owner, ass knows the way to its master's crib." It is possible that the Roman liturgist also knew pseudo-Matthew, who mentions the animals adoring him (M. Chapter 14).

The final offspring of the Christmas psalter was a series for Virgins developed by the Roman breviary. Here, too, an order of twelve in the form gives rise to the suspicion that a Benedictine series of twelve psalms is the connecting link:

B. V. M.:   8 18 23 44 45 47 71 84 86 95 96 97
Roman B. V. M.: 8 18 23 44 45
Roman Virg.:   8 18 23 44 45 47

The difference between the two series is clear. In the Office of Virgins Ps. 86 is missing. The reason for this is obvious. The markedly Marian character of the psalm was realized and, therefore, it had to be excluded. The fact that Ps. 47 is found in its stead is most easily understood if the series of nine is an immediate offshoot of a Benedictine series of twelve. The choice of Ps. 47 has, therefore, no particular bearing on the feast of Virgins. On the contrary, it seems to have been overlooked that the psalm is taken from the Christmas psalter and was probably put there because of the position of the Nativity shrine on the Esquiline hill. Unfortunately, most of the antiphons are not taken from the psalms and are, therefore, excluded as far as an interpretation is concerned.

Both series, the one for the Blessed Virgin and the one for Virgins, come from Benedictine series. Originally the Virgins, since they were all martyrs, were given the psalter for Martyrs. Even the twelfth century antiphonary of St. Peter, B. 79, does not do otherwise and offers the above series only for St. Mary Magdalene. In the present Breviary St. Agatha has the psalter for Martyrs, St. Cecilia, on the other hand, has the series for Virgins, and St. Agnes a combination from both:

1 2 3 4 5 8 14 44 45

The endeavour to reach a liturgically proper understanding of the different series dealt with here is, at the same time, an attempt to achieve true prayer. If it is not possible in every case to establish exactly the reason for the choice of psalms, it must be borne in mind that in many cases this is decided entirely by some special situation at the outset, as, for example, the factors connected with the Church of St. Mary Major. For this reason an investigation of the initial situation is often hopeless. Then everything is left to the free response of the heart in prayer and song and this remains the be-all and end-all of psalmody.

6

Holy Week
The Focal Point of Liturgical Work

Eugen Walter

A Letter

Dear Brother in Christ,

I am aware that you feel increasingly harassed by the Easter ceremonies and I understand this feeling. It is increasingly difficult to shut your mind to the realization that you will have to deal quite differently with this matter; and you are, at the same time, worried – not to say fearful – about how you can succeed in doing so with the resources at your disposal.

A feeling of anxiety is no bad preparation. This cause merits it. In fact, it is due to such an anxiety that the liturgical revision of the Easter ceremonies has come about. There cannot, then, be any better starting-point for their proper performance and ordering than this first initially creative dissatisfaction which was the source of the reform. Not only should you not avoid it, you should even encourage it and, what is more, communicate it to your parish! Indeed, the parish too, should share your dissatisfaction. Except for and second only to your own dissatisfaction, I know of no better preparation for the next Easter ceremonies than this profound and active concern of the parish.

Do not say that it is no good suggesting this sort of thing. You underestimate your parish. And even though you could with justice point to the apathy and dullness which you already experienced innumerable times, yet, nonetheless, there is another equally real side which you have simply not taken into account and it is up to you whether you utilize it as a positive help or let it grow to a smouldering discontent. I mean that no parish is hermetically sealed off at its boundaries. Your parish is a member of the community as a whole, a member of the Church. What has reached fruition in the larger community, is not sterile in the individual parish. You can learn this from experience, just as innumerable priests have done already, although at first they too only groaned: "But that's unthinkable for my parish!" – only to observe with complete astonishment how, quite as a matter of course, the faithful could do such a lot at a first attempt. This is, moreover, true not only of country districts; it holds good for many town churches and suburban parishes with fluctuating congregations where practices cannot be held beforehand – and yet the fact is that thousands were able to sing the appropriate plainsong Mass "at sight". Admittedly, not every individual would have been able to do so by himself, but in becoming part of the community in and through the sacred ceremonies, each discovered the ability which was communicated by the individuals to the whole and from the whole to the individuals. The ability was communicated, because the will was there too. Ultimately ability and will are the same thing. If you succeed in giving the impulse to the will, then the ability to do anything is, at most, only a question of time.

So it is in your case, too, dear Brother in Christ. If you intend not to shelve the matter any longer, then you will see that it is a lot easier than you now think and fear.

What is it all about? It is about the Easter ceremonies of the

Church. We say "ceremonies" and, in doing so, employ a much-used word, but here we use it in a fuller, truer sense; indeed, I think I may say, in the truest sense. A special High Mass before the Blessed Sacrament exposed, accompanied by all possible pomp for all the senses, may be "ceremonious" – it would be far from approaching the Easter "ceremonies" in our sense. Why is this? It is because such a display of splendour can take place on any feast; it has nothing specifically to do with Easter. It is not the array of such aids to magnificence which makes Easter the archetype of all Christian ceremonial feasts. It is because the Church, (that is, the living active community) is co-enacting the pasch of her Lord, the journey through the Passion to the winning of new life. This passage through the Passion to glory is not only the historical source of our Redemption, it remains the permanent condition and form of its application to ourselves. The deeper we involve ourselves in participation in the Passion of the Lord, the more we win a share in his life. To put it another way: here the way is open to anyone who wishes to share more fully in the Kingdom of Christ. This is what the symbolism of every sacrament tells us, for every sacrament contains in symbols a reference to the death of the Lord, but, above all, the two principal sacraments, Baptism and the Eucharist.

According to St. Paul (Rom. 6), we are redeemed and made Christians by experiencing in ourselves the Death and Resurrection of our Lord in the mystery of Baptism. Because this sacrament can, however, only be received once, there is the Eucharist, through which the repetition of this mystery is made possible for us: "as often as ye shall do these things, ye shall proclaim the death of the Lord." Since, however, it is

74

again impossible for us to co-enact the whole event in spirit, as is "meet and just", through frequent repetition within the brief course of a Mass, there are therefore the Easter ceremonies, in which all the events of our Salvation, of three days, are spread out before us to their proper extent and at their proper intensity. In the unparalleled ceremonies of these three days everything comes before us in turn and seems to be actually happening, so that we are really gripped by it. And here we come to the point: it is in this process that we comprehend our salvation and are at the same time comprehended by it.

Here I may, perhaps, draw attention to an experience in pastoral work which has probably caused you trouble often enough: on the one hand, a generally over-abstract concept of salvation among our faithful or an over-concrete concept of grace; and, on the other hand, conclusions drawn from their idea of grace, which are too much concerned with specific moral requirements. A mind informed by Christ and a way of life modelled on Christ do not automatically result from a state of grace. If, however, we ask ourselves how Jesus instructed his disciples, how he revealed to them the inner meaning of grace, we have to answer: through their contact with him, through lingering in his presence, through living with him. This is precisely what these holy days enable us to do, if they are properly used. They bring us into a unique intimacy with our Lord, they allow our inner senses to be filled and formed by it, so that without a doubt more happens within us during these days than we ourselves can realize. In this way the gap which we detected between "abstract grace" and our material life and its claims is filled. The thing which was lacking is precisely the intermediary effect of our contact with the Lord and of our

75

commitment to him. For this reason it is also important that the parish's celebration should involve them in an active participation. In brief, we can now say that the concept of "celebration" covers both sides, the active and the passive. It is, in fact, impossible really to separate one from the other. The only possibility is to start from the position of an existing separation in order to overcome it. Only in so far as the state of atrophy can be overcome can we speak once again of true celebration.

Worship is not only a prerequisite for and a means of receiving grace; in it take place the fundamental acts of the new life. Through the co-enactment of the sacred ceremony the bonds of torpor which bind the inner powers of the soul are loosened. And this happens to the extent that a real co-enactment of the sacred ceremony takes place. That active participation, at which all the Popes Pius of our century have aimed, forms part of it. For them it is certainly not just a question of another liturgical style or an ideal unearthed from previous centuries. For them it is a question of the salvation of souls or, more precisely and comprehensively, of the salvation of the world. And here they recognize the key position for this. No call to the apostolate, no activating of the laity can bear fruit, if the parishes do not find life in the one thing which feeds the life of Christ in us. The call of the Popes has been heard for a long time in general terms, but it has now moved to the point which is the pivot. No feast in the Church's year is more appropriate, none is more necessary than the feast of Easter. In the commandment about Easter communion something of the importance of the Easter feast was preserved. This was, however, not enough to make everyone conscious of the fact that the yearly feast of Easter is nothing less than the annual re-initiation into being a Christian.

For the large majority of the faithful the great catechumenical instruction of the Lenten Masses was entirely lost, because for them Easter was only the Resurrection of the Lord and not at the same time their own resurrection conceived in faith and sealed in the sacrament. This is why, through the reform of the Easter Vigil, this feeling of shock and of personal involvement is now so important. And we priests and pastors have to see that in our performance of the Easter ceremonies this real participation is experienced by each one of the faithful.

Before I now pass on to practical suggestions, I should like to mention a few general principles which are based on my own experience and which I feel will give you encouragement.

It is impossible for everything to succeed perfectly the first year. It is quite impossible to begin everything all at once. It is a question of making a good beginning – that is, a beginning on which you can build in the years to come. In order to do this, you need to provide yourself with a note-book in which you can write down how things went after every service – and how they could be improved next year. It is immediately after the ceremony that you have the clearest impression of the way in which you would have wished it to be better and of how you can best avoid this or that mistake. In the course of the year this note-book will become your best external aid. There will, indeed, always be something which you wish were better, but the most important thing is that you are able to observe how the parish is gradually growing together and that they and their celebration are becoming more and more a living entity; that the individual rites are not only performed correctly but become closer to our hearts and, in a good sense, more and more a matter of course.

Let us now discuss the possibilities for the individual days, which together make up the Paschal festival.

Palm Sunday

Here it will be essential to discuss the preparations which concern the celebrant alone. What is the whole point as far as the ceremony is concerned? Surely it is the homage which is prepared for the Messiah by his community. One must, then, make this homage possible.

In our parish, too, we have no processional route other than out of the church (by the side-door on the right), round the church yard and back in by the main door. So to us, too, it seemed impracticable to have the whole congregation walking in the procession (similarly, they cannot all receive the palms one by one). On the day when the *pueri Hebraeorum* duly hailed the Messiah with hosannas, it is above all the youth of the parish who should be active. In Germany we even take this as an opportunity to include the school-leavers formally in a service. Since the majority of children continue with a higher education, there would be too few boys and girls leaving to put them by themselves in a place of honour in front of the congregation for a special service, There is, however, a unique opportunity to address a few telling words to them and to the young people who belong to the various parish organizations, after they have received their palms and are standing among the congregation before the priest: "In the same way as we now go out of the church with one another and with Christ into this part of the world, so should you go out into life to conquer and reform the world for Christ, so that you may one day

78

enter into the heavenly Jerusalem at the great triumphant celebration, the likeness of which we now commemorate." We do
not let the children join in – although of course they would
gladly do so – since the young people would then no longer
wish to take part in the way that they do. With these young
people it is possible to rehearse the distribution or receiving
of the palms beforehand and also a hosanna chorus (vernacular
or Latin) which should be as simple as possible; in the same way
the church choir can prepare a similar or a different one, so
that even the first year a refreshing variety is obtained. The
second year one can easily invite the congregation to say or sing
the hosanna with the choir. And rest assured: they do sing! As
we enter the church we have a hymn to Christ the King sung as
a climax. There is, then, not much to prepare. What is all-
important, is that the whole thing should have vitality. Important, too, are a few explanatory words from the priest. I prefer
to speak after the distribution of the palms, because then the
young people are still in a group, standing ready for the procession, their attention at its peak. And it seems to me to be necessary for them to have some guidance so that they feel the reality
of what they are about to do. The short address could, of course,
also take place after the return to the altar. Everyone will have
to sense for himself at what point in the proceedings he has to
help the participants by his words to a real co-operation. There
is reason to do this twice on Palm Sunday: once to make the
ceremony itself into a true act of homage and then to tell the
parish that the great ceremonies of Holy Week have now begun,
that every day has its mystery and that what matters is that each
person should co-operate in the great ceremonies of our Redemption to the best of his ability.

Maundy Thursday

Id est hodie – on this evening it is not difficult to bring the congregation to an awareness of the witnessed truth of this "today". Therefore no outer display need be used. The unique character of this Mass must spring simply from within, while we, by our words, help the community to be fully present.

There is no reason why the Washing of the Feet should not be attempted. I know of no case where such a venture has miscarried. People have only mentioned the opposite: great emotion on the part of participants and congregation. It is only necessary to explain this rite as a representation; watching with real attention is the most important act of participation in what Jesus did for each of his apostles and would wish to do for each one of us now called to his supper. Details then become unimportant. We should see Our Lord in the priest and in the twelve men representatives of the whole parish. Each year there should be a different twelve so that all personal interest becomes unimportant.

As you know, various criteria have been suggested with regard to the choice of the twelve men. As far as I am concerned, I take care to have the whole parish represented: two men from the Blessed Sacrament Guild, two from the choir or two who give service to the church in some other way, then two men of good standing and at least two not of good standing in the sense of 1 Cor. 1:5. I leave them in their places in the nave until after the homily, in which I tell the congregation how to participate as spectators, then they rise and come into the choir. The places and positions have been briefly discussed the day before, so that everyone knows the route he has to take and the seat where he has to sit. Apart from this, it is better that everything should take place without constraint rather than be carried out in a studied manner.

Even when the distribution of Holy Communion lasts a long time – as it does today and on Good Friday and at the Mass of the Easter Vigil – we prefer not to shorten or fill in the time by having hymn-singing throughout. The silence of these days is the purest that there is and it should not be obscured. It is also easier for the majority of communicants to concentrate in their prayer on these days than at any other time.

Good Friday

Next come the two days on which one cannot satisfactorily hold the service without a reader. It would be a pity if the priest read the two prophecies only in Latin and it would be impossible within the time available to read them one after the other in Latin and in the vernacular. It is therefore necessary to obtain the services of a reader or, better, two – it is probably easier, in fact, to obtain two rather than just one. In case of necessity one can call upon older servers and this also solves the question of liturgical clothing in the easiest way; for not every man or youth will willingly put on cassock and cotta. While the priest reads the lesson quietly in Latin at the sedilia, in order to satisfy the regulations, the reader reads it aloud in English. The prayers, too, can be said by him or by another reader; we prefer to have the priest sing the Latin text here so that the difference between the lesson and the prayer is not obscured and the function of the priest stands out more clearly.

One can deal in a similar way with the Solemn Prayers of intercession. This is even facilitated by the fact that the actual prayers only sum up what has been expanded in the prefaces, which would then be read out by the reader.

The Passion should at least be read, if not sung, with the parts allotted to different men; where three singers are available it is better to have it sung.

In our parish the whole congregation takes part in the Veneration of the Cross. The men and women come forward for it as naturally as they later do to receive Holy Communion. We do, however, restrict ourselves to one genuflection.

The choir should not sing throughout at this point, even if it is the popular and beautiful *Improperia* by Vittoria. The congregation should be made accustomed to the idea of how very expressive silence can be.

We have a simplified vernacular version of the antiphon: "We adore thy Cross, O Lord: and we praise and glorify thy holy Resurrection." The first year we had it printed and duplicated with the melody. Now it is sufficient for the choir to sing it the first time, then the congregation sing it from memory after them, every three times at a higher pitch.

Easter Eve

We have always made a point of seeing that even this greatest and richest part of the liturgy does not last more than two hours. It is possible to achieve this and still carry through everything not only in a dignified manner but also meaningfully and have all available priests distributing Communion for a good quarter of an hour. Admittedly, it all needs good preparation. This consists, to a great extent, in the celebrant's having thought everything out properly and having everything down to the last detail firmly in mind in the light of his previous experience; and, secondly, in his giving very precise directions in his practice with the altar-servers, so that later during the ceremony a slight reminder is sufficient for them to perform the proper action or duty. They should know exactly at what points the threefold *Lumen Christi* is to be sung and what follows each (lighting of candles after the second, taking the light to the faithful after the third; regarding this latter point, they should each know at what bench they are to begin), so that everything takes place in an orderly manner, swiftly and yet calmly. Before or after the practice (or both) it is a good idea to talk it over again individually with those servers who have important duties, so that they feel particularly responsible for the smooth running of the ceremonies and so can really relieve the celebrant of a great deal of worry. In the main the successful outcome depends upon us priests, however many people are working with us. If it is successful, an inner harmony and peace will radiate to the congregation from each individual part of the ceremony. For this to happen, the priest has to tune well his rich instrument of assistants and their functions. There is plenty of time to do this in twenty-four hours.

The *Exsultet* forms the first climax of the night's ceremonies. In the wealth of the motifs which are struck, in the poetic and musical vitality of the text, it is the true Easter song of exultation. What good is this, however, if the conditions for bringing a fair section of the congregation to an understanding of it are lacking? Not every deacon or priest possesses a good voice, nor every member of the congregation a text in the vernacular which is readable by candlelight. For this reason, practical considerations which will cleverly take into account what is available and what can be attained are indispensable. Even when the deacon is sufficiently musical the parish-priest must weigh up whether he would not do his congregation and their Easter celebration a greater service if he sang only a part in Latin and said the rest. The Blessing of the Water (which ranks even higher) seems to authorize such a change. It would also be possible to have it all read out in the vernacular while the priest or deacon said the Latin text. A lot depends on the way the text is read. It is on what a reader can make of it that the decision, whether to shorten the text rather than let its length become tiresome, is taken.

One should have at least two readers for the four Lessons – a change of voices is a great relief when listening to so many texts. This applies even more if the celebrant prefers to have the prayers too read in the vernacular.

It would be justifiable, too, to have the reader give a synopsis of the Lessons (especially the second to the fourth) instead of singing them, followed by the synopsis of the Prayers, so that the priest can sing the Latin text of the Prayer after the few moments for silent prayer.

It is the custom in many places to have the Litany of the Saints sung in Latin and the responses sung by the congregation, because everything in it can be understood quite easily and this litany, as the oldest, has a particularly venerable tradition. (This is not, however, meant as a criticism of those who decide on using the vernacular version.)

At the Blessing of the Water it is certainly possible – and for

84

the priest who has to do everything without help sometimes necessary vocally – to increase the parts which are prescribed to be read and not sung.

An actual administration of the sacrament of Baptism begins with the words: N., do you believe ...; the rite up to this point is carried out in private beforehand (if possible by the same priest who is administering the baptism). For the Renewal of Baptismal Promises an impressive assembly of all the assistants and ministers towards the people should be arranged. A few introductory words by the parish-priest before the prescribed liturgical text will ensure it a more attentive reception. For the High Mass which follows there is, of course, nothing better than Plainsong Mass I; the polyphonic Mass is more suited to the High Mass during the day. If you have courage enough for the attempt and do not ask too much all at once, you will soon find that the whole congregation joins in the singing. The necessary beginning is first for the church choir to learn the Mass and then for several groups who have the opportunity for one or two practices to learn it too (the young people and women, for instance). They will manage the *Kyrie* and *Sanctus* in a few short practices. If they do not get as far as the Gloria the first year, you will still discover that during and through the ceremony itself they can all manage a lot more, although no-one quite knows how.

With these groups the triple Alleluia after the Epistle and the Alleluia antiphon at Lauds can also be prepared. In general, at this Mass, whose unusual character (no *Credo,* Offertory, *Agnus Dei,* Communion or Last Gospel) is not only preserved but emphasized by the new rite, the moments of silence should not be disturbed by singing. The choir could sing something well-

85

chosen or the organist play during the distribution of Communion. But a certain restraint should remain which is not completely dispelled till Easter Day itself.

Regarding Easter candles a choice has to be made from the many available candles and the place and method of their distribution to the faithful determined: it is best to do this at the church door (with the accessories, particularly protective cases against the wind to prevent dripping on to the benches). Perhaps the young people might take on the decorating of candles with Easter symbols for themselves and for the sick.

The Easter water presents even more of a headache. People seem to think more easily of bringing candles than containers for the water. We have acquired a quantity of medicine bottles, which we have had painted with symbols by the young people, and give these out with the candles for a few pence.

When can the necessary practices be held?

Let us presume that we have a parish of which no practices, as such, can be demanded. The evening devotions on the Sundays of Lent and, in particular, the Lenten sermons will be attended by a nucleus of the parish and with this nucleus it is possible to practise for five or ten minutes at the start or finish. The necessary texts can be duplicated and laid out ready.

What can and should be practised? Not absolutely everything the first year! 1. A Hosanna for Palm Sunday. 2. The *Venite adoremus* for Good Friday, and perhaps the Resurrection antiphon; the Our Father in Latin. 3. The opening acclamations at the Blessing of the Paschal Candle and of the Baptismal Water (here the decision has to be made whether to insist on the use of the ferial tone, when it will probably not be used elsewhere). 4. The above-mentioned triple Alleluia. 5. The plainsong Mass I.

After Easter

Anyone who has taken trouble with the Easter ceremonies is not happy until he has passed, as if through a rough sea, through all this stress and strain and reached the release of the Easter feast itself. This is right and proper. But can and should he let the matter rest there? Should the faithful now be left to themselves? It would be wrong, as it is wrong with the first communicants, to let everything drop after that Sunday. An important indication is given by the fact that the Church continues the intensity of the daily Masses throughout the octave of Easter; the Prayers of the whole octave deserve particular attention: their constant plea is that we may keep and show in our lives what we have just celebrated. A devoted priest will help his parish to do this. Even when they do not come to Mass daily, he must remind them that they have been born again by their celebration of Easter and make sure that they remain aware of this rebirth. For most people only Sunday provides an opportunity of doing this. But this is precisely the meaning of the Christian Sunday! And the Christian communities must be directed anew into its true celebration at our present time, in which the meaning of Sunday has by and large disappeared.

7

Liturgical Education for School-leavers

Ferdinand Krenzer

At first sight religion would seem to have a limited appeal to young people between the ages of 14 and 17. On the other hand, we can see that the time when children are leaving secondary school is precisely one which presents us with a favourable opportunity which we should be unwise to neglect. In the months before they leave school, boys and girls show a great interest in everything connected with the world outside. This means that if religious "school-leaving days" are organized, interest in them is always relatively high. This is particularly the case if young people can see even from the invitations that they are no longer being addressed as school-children, that the questions they want to put are important, and that an attempt is being made to bridge the gap between school and the life ahead of them. The young people will then attend a course of talks for school-leavers regularly, even when it lasts for several months. One of our boys who hardly ever went to church said: "These talks are the most sensible thing there is in the parish."

Where it is feasible one should not dispense with this instruction, which extends over a period of months, in favour of one day of recollection. It would be ideal to have both. In my experience, the effects of anything up to three days of recollection soon wear off and at their age it is too much to expect young people to practise spiritual exercises in the strict sense. One of the advantages of a longer period of instruction is that it allows one to keep back a certain boy or girl, whom one otherwise rarely sees, on several different occasions after instruction for personal conversation; another is that over a longer period of time one can draw the attention of the group to a particular point, until something akin to a fresh start can be detected in one or other of them. Suggestions leading to religious action are precisely those which cannot be given in the course of one day, however rich in experience; they need time and, at this age, a certain care in handling too. Here we have in front of us boys and girls with whom we may have had no contact for several years; they come of their own free will, attracted by themes and topics which appeal to them.

At all events, religious education at this age should be entirely focused on action and any theorizing avoided. Here lies both our opportunity and our difficulty in giving essentially liturgical instruction to this age-group. Our opportunity, since the liturgy is, after all, religious practice; our difficulty, since our liturgical forms have no longer any meaning in themselves and can only be made comprehensible in the light of historical, theoretical and intellectual considerations. Our signs and symbols are not taken from the imaginative world of the young people of today, though the latter is by no means devoid of symbols. We must therefore have the courage to be selective. At this age-level there are three religious topics – besides other more biological ones – which must definitely be dealt with in detail: prayer, confession and the Mass. The first two ("I can't pray" and "Why and how should I make my confession?") are inherent concerns of this age-group; this is proved

89

by the fact that these topics always make for a successful discussion, indeed that they arouse even greater interest than the usual box-office successes. It is more difficult to introduce the subject of the Mass, although they all complain: "I don't seem to be able to get on with it."

Prayer

Prayer is not simply something *I* do – this important fact should, it seems to me, be brought home to young people. It is important, too, for the later instruction on the Mass. "What do I get out of it?" and "Praying doesn't help" are the catch-phrases young people will often use as excuses. It would be a first important step to show that prayer is still meaningful even when we "don't feel like it" – that we keep on with it simply because it is so "meet and just" – and, above all, to show how prayer in this situation can look quite practical. Here, admittedly, lies the first difficulty, because at this age there is scarcely any real sense of duty.

After this it is a question of leading them on to "adult" prayer without breaking any good habits. Otherwise many young people think that the childish form is something which is automatically part of anything religious. This later leads to rejection. Thus we must lead them from formal prayer to conversation, to a personal relationship. To be able to speak to God, one must first create the necessary condition for it: concentration. How? – But what if I can't concentrate, because one particular thought keeps running through my head? Then make your start from whatever is occupying your mind, the

90

joy, anger, guilt which fills you at that moment. The "prayer for all life's situations" is the most necessary and the most needed one for this age. To try to talk to them at length about contemplative prayer would be a wasted effort as far as the majority of young people are concerned. The objection: "But what when nothing comes into my head?" must be dealt with. Perhaps in answer to this question it is best to show what prayer in fact is, the number of things with which prayer can be linked, and what a prayer would be like in these circumstances. For it is precisely this lack of ideas which is my complaint to the Lord. In this situation, however, when they have no ideas at all, it is a good thing for young people to know set prayers too. Therefore these should not suffer by their being educated in personal prayer. The young people must realize too, that in this case it does not show a lack of resourcefulness but, in fact, intelligence to dip into a good prayer-book. Above all, at this age nothing should be given up, unless an equally valid or better substitute is found.

The Mass

What has been said, by way of introduction, about prayer is even more true as far as the Mass is concerned. Here the objection runs: The Mass gives me nothing, I only sit through it. What above all is worth while explaining, is that my feelings are not all-important, that simply being there and giving up my time is important to God, that God can make demands on me.

Apart from this there are difficulties which arise concerning the Mass, which do not exist with personal prayer: first of all the set form, which one simply has to accept and make one's own; but the biggest difficulty consists in the fact that the youth of today has little connection with the community, for the good reason that it scarcely knows any valid forms of community. Quite apart from the rites, which are difficult to understand, the praise of God in the community is something which is no longer so easily comprehensible as it was in earlier times, when life ran its course entirely within the communities of family and village.

Everywhere where young people celebrate Mass in an environment which they feel to be a real community – for instance, in a youth camp – this difficulty perceptibly diminishes and disappears. In any case it seems extremely doubtful whether young people of this age really should be forced to sit in the front benches (as is the practice in Germany) when there is a general Communion for the parish. However desirable this might be, they do not see why they should go there. As far as many of them are concerned, we must feel satisfied when they are there at all.

When, in the face of these difficulties, one has only two hours at one's disposal to treat the subject of the Mass, it is necessary to omit all liturgical details. The first concern should be to explain what the Mass is: sacrifice, meal, commemoration. One of these essential interpretations can form the bridge to the idea of the communion of the faithful. Finally some help should be given as regards an appropriate personal disposition and co-celebration; for example, attention to the sermon, reflections and prayers at the Offertory. In this way the objection that the Mass is boring will be disposed of at the same time. The young person needs aids to prevent it becoming boring, aids into which he himself can introduce variations: how to join in, instruction in the different ways of participating and the different views of prayer, on the Liturgical Year, or on other ideas which may run through the text of the Mass or the sermon.

A particular problem of this age-group is the transition from the Children's Mass, common in many places, to the Community Mass. In my experience young people still cling to the children's service because it is usually pleasant and makes no demands on them in its sermon or its form, and often, too, because of its shortness. Anyone who has not, up till then, assisted at High Mass, will find it difficult to accustom himself to it. The transition is correspondingly easier for servers and choir, providing that membership does not lapse on leaving school. For all the others, however, the transition between the children's Mass and that for young people should take place not after leaving school, but now, at the same time as the lessons of instruction, six months before leaving school. At such a time one can still give guidance, can still clear up misunderstandings, meet objections and also exercise a certain control. "You belong with the adults" is something they are not unpleased to hear. If they accustom themselves at this stage to the adult community, a break will perhaps be avoided altogether.

It is best if special Masses can be said for the young people. Then they feel themselves to be a community. This would be the best way of preserving a love of and desire for the Mass amongst the more willing. Something that has been arranged especially for them, usually has a powerful appeal. Then they do not stand at the back but take a part in it. And one often hears them say: "Today I really managed to pray again!"

Educating them towards a regular attendance would also be important. Boys and girls are often accustomed to seeing the opposite in their parents. Here we are once more back at our starting-point, the idea of duty. A duty does not have to appeal to me. Time and again young people make a new flying start during this time, especially in response to personal appeals.

Confession

As I have already said, the subject of confession is easier to handle. It is considered as more interesting. Probably this is because Confession is usually imagined to be something completely subjective, something completely private between God and the individual. This fits in well with the subjectivity of the young. Here, however, lies the first difficulty. For here too the community must be brought into view.

This may be a difficult task with this age-group. But it is, none-theless, essential. Later, the moment will certainly come when confession does not offer one much from the subjective point of view, when feelings do not come into it at all. Then, all too easily, going to confession is dropped. The consciousness that guilt is no private concern, that confession as a sacrament is an outstanding way of honouring God, that here too it is not a question of how I feel and that here too God has a claim, may help them later on.

Sometimes when we listen to talks on confession we gain the impression that what we have done up till then, and the way we have done it, has been quite mistaken. Young people, how-ever, do not at their age want to begin again from the beginning. Any development should not create the impression that the priest will not be satisfied with them if they confess in the old way. It should rather awaken joy in confession (in so far as this is no contradiction). It is just the person who goes rarely to confession, who will later no longer remember what it is he ought to do differently and will therefore prefer to stay away entirely rather than do something "wrong".

In spite of this, it is an important matter to encourage development in confession. Later they will certainly no longer be satisfied with the children's form and thus drift away from the Sacrament of Penance. The basic tone of the instruction regarding confession should be: The way in which you did it up till now was quite right, but here, as everywhere else, you must now be adult.

I am here trying to face the difficulties which arise in this age-group. They are, in fact, partly rooted in dissatisfaction with the children's form. Starting from these difficulties, the essential truths can be pointed out too.

The first difficulty, which is invariably mentioned when one enquires about it, is "You have to *tell* your sins", that is, the difficulty of expressing something embarrassing. But the difficulty lies, in fact, not in expressing, but in recognizing it, in the examination of conscience. No-one likes admitting that there is something wrong with him. This is the embarrassing thing. The expressing of it is then often a necessity (guilt complexes). Another objection which has to be dealt with is: "Why have aural confession anyway?"

Next: "It is always the same." Behind this lies annoyance with the eternal sameness of our self-accusations (the famous analogy of the gramophone record). This is due partly to the nature of things (everyone has typical faults) but also partly to the way in which we confess. Try doing it differently for once! Try to explain less and to describe more (without becoming long-

95

winded)! In spite of this, a fixed form at least at beginning and end should not be abandoned. Admittedly, one should indicate the possibility of confessing without any set form, of simply saying, for instance: "Help me, please . . ." For some this will one day provide a bridge.

The objection: "I don't see any progress" is an extension of the above difficulty. In this case encouraging a more searching examination of conscience is effective. Not just to recognize my faults but to get at the roots: my chief failing? Expressed in negative terms: where would I be without confession? Here perhaps many mistakes have been made, particularly regarding failures in sexual matters. The phrase "Confession will help you out of it" is, at the very least, open to misunderstanding and can occasion bitter disappointments.

"I cannot find anything to confess. I haven't done anything so very bad." Why confess so often? Behind this may lie the wide-spread presumption, which is unwilling to admit any guilt. In this case the assessment might be taken further: What good have I omitted to do?

"Always the same boring exhortation!" But if you will confess in a personal way, you will receive personal words of advice; otherwise the priest is forced to remain general. Age and perhaps job could be indicated!

"Perhaps the priest knows me." "What will he think of me?" Here one should indicate the possibility, which exists almost everywhere, of avoiding any particular priest, but one should also show how personal guidance can best help someone to progress.

If one starts in this way from the objections it does not turn into a boring lecture. The young people are conscious of their

questions being answered. Giving examples presents one difficulty. It is advisable only to use examples which you have in-
vented and to say so explicitly.

The important thing at this age is: to keep practice alive. It is
valuable to impress upon young people that in spite of their
difficulties of belief or their lack of interest they should hold
firmly to certain religious practices and carry them out in good
faith, even if, for the time being, they feel no urge to do so.
Depth comes in time. At this stage nothing should be thrown
away. Prayer, confession, the Sacrifice of the Mass are positions
not to be relinquished. To succeed in preventing them from
letting everything lapse, in making their observance easy and,
if possible, in giving them some pleasure in it, is to succeed as
far as is possible at this stage of their lives.

8

The Children's Mass

HENRY FISCHER

THE Liturgical Movement of our time has re-opened our eyes
to the people's participation in the celebration of the Holy Sacrifice of the Mass. To 'attend' Mass, to 'hear' Mass devoutly, to
'assist' at Mass, indeed even 'to pray the Mass' are thus expressions of an education in and attitude towards the Mass which
sound wrong to us today. We know that the Holy Sacrifice of
the Mass was given to us, above all, that it might be *our* sacrifice, which we offer and co-celebrate in and through Christ to
the heavenly Father. Priest and people, that is the Church, are
incorporated by the celebration of Mass into the sacrifice of
Christ and enter actively into it. His sacrifice becomes our
sacrifice not only in word but through our action. Our participation is thus not limited to "hearing", "assisting", "praying" –
though it is all these too – but is a matter of real joint celebration of an *actio eucharistica*. This is in no way meant to refer
only to the celebrant, but rather to involve the whole jointly
celebrating community. Admittedly there is a type of *actio*
which belongs to the celebrant alone but this is not to say
that the whole *actio* of the Mass is therefore restricted to
him. A real joint-celebration belongs to the people also and
this is not fulfilled by a passive "being present". All instruction on the Mass must, then, have as its aim, that of leading

the faithful to a true joint-celebration of the Eucharistic Sacrifice.

The order, the rite, the ceremonial form of the Holy Sacrifice of the Mass given to us in its liturgy are also full of this idea. From this rediscovery of the liturgical form of the Mass we have through the Liturgical Movement really come up against the essential content of the Eucharistic Sacrifice. Because the Sacrifice of the Mass is the celebration of the Church, because the Church is a community, a cult is necessary which confronts the individual objectively and to which the individual with his subjective powers can subscribe. In other words, the real joint-celebration of the Eucharistic Sacrifice must be a liturgical co-celebration. The invention from time to time of a subjective form of co-celebration – which basically can be envisaged in innumerable variations – must mean a departure from the real nature of the celebration itself, if these forms have not been taken up and endorsed by the community and its authority as belonging to it. The "liturgical jungle", as a great many subjective experiments have sometimes been described, is a contradiction in terms. A true education in the Sacrifice of the Mass must aim at the introduction of the faithful to the liturgical co-celebration of the Eucharistic Sacrifice.

Here we touch on the fundamental problem of our subject: how can we introduce children to a real liturgical co-celebration of the Mass without doing harm to the psychology of the child? In other words, how can we achieve a real liturgical co-celebration of the Mass which is, nonetheless, suited to children? Although there is no children's liturgy for the Mass, nonetheless the children's joint-celebration can and must be completely in harmony with a child's psyche.

Two mistaken solutions have often been put forward. One consists in thinking that, even for children, instruction on the Sacrifice of the Mass in the spirit of the liturgy must necessarily begin with the liturgical form of the Mass. In fact this was historically the way taken by the Liturgical Movement. But this is not a wise beginning for children. Too often the final product is a liturgically well "functioning" school-Mass, in which the children have mastered the 'technique' of the liturgical action, without, however, having made the vital move beyond the form to the content of the Eucharistic act of oblation. On the contrary, the effort to follow the outer liturgical action as closely as possible – and for children this is complicated – can so absorb (and tire) the child's powers of comprehension that any response and receptivity for an inner enactment of the sacrifice are quite blunted. It does not seem a good idea to aim at a child's using the Ordinary of the Mass from the Missal by the time of its First Communion, not to mention following the variable parts of the Mass.

The other false solution is one which holds it possible to become quite independent of the liturgical form, so that two parallel celebrations result: that of the priest at the altar and that of the children. Since the objective form of the liturgy is felt to be very little suited to children, it is thought possible to abandon it in favour of a children's Mass which runs parallel. I do not mean the previous type of "Mass devotions" which held that any type of devotion (the Rosary, litanies to St. Joseph or the Angels and so on) was permissible during the celebration of the Mass. This view should have been quite superseded by now. There is, however, a type of Mass devotions which attempts to make the dogmatic, ascetic and even liturgical content of the Mass accessible to children and yet does not perceive its unity with the celebration of the priest at the altar, as Karl Rahner has recently noted. Not once is the dialogue between priest and congregation taken into consideration. The catechetical preoccupation here pushes the liturgical celebration unwarrantably into the background. This is sometimes taken so far that the Mass is used as an occasion for explaining Mass rubrics.

All the difficulties of this question spring from the discrepancy which is felt between the objective liturgical Mass-form and the requirements of an arrangement of the Mass and the teaching on it which is suited to children. – The difficulties inherent in the liturgy are generally known: the unfamiliarity of its language and the frequent incomprehensibility of its prayers for the majority of children. On the other hand the liturgy itself offers important aids towards the arrangement of the celebration in a way suited to children. Klemens Tilmann demonstrates this convincingly for the highest form of the Mass liturgy, the plainsong Mass, when he suggests that the liturgy meets the child's need for variation, stimulates devotion, has a clear and consistent pattern, nourishes private prayer and reflection and is visual in its presentation.[1] Nonetheless the problem of "transposition" still exists. The elements enumerated above, which are taken from the liturgy, can of course make the co-celebration of Mass profoundly fruitful for children, but for this they have to be transposed. – The greatest difficulty, however, seems to us to arise from the teaching about the Mass. The traditional Mass teaching, which has been given for generations (and still is given) to children in schools, moves on lines which make a true com-

[1] Klemens Tilmann in: *Eucharistie und Katechese,* Freiburg 1958, pp. 104 ff.

101

prehension of the Sacrifice of the Mass and of an active participation in it almost impossible.

Some of the elements of this traditional teaching on the Mass
may be sketched briefly. It represents the Mass as the scene of the
"coming down of Jesus" at the consecration. The Lord as our
Mediator and his presence in the priest from the beginning of the
Eucharistic celebration and the heavenly Father as the real
person addressed in the celebration are ignored. In the light of
this teaching, the Mass is not worship but a means of worship.
It is the means of procuring the sacramental presence of Jesus,
it is the means of procuring (of 'making present') Christ's
Sacrifice on the cross so that we may share in its fruits, finally
it is the means of procuring Holy Communion. The last, too,
is seen quite independently of the sacrificial act, not as fruit of
the sacrifice nor as the ultimate union of self with the Sacrifice
of Christ, but exclusively as the visit of the Heavenly Guest and
the Jesus-mysticism with which this is surrounded. It must be
understood that where such teaching on the Mass prevails, the
basic understanding necessary for a co-enactment, for an
active participation in the Eucharistic celebration is not awakened
at all. What is more, this basic understanding is directly ham-
pered by such teaching. In recent years, however, the following curious development seems to have taken place: under
the influence of the Liturgical Movement the attempt has been
made to explain to children too the liturgical form of the Mass
and to have them take part in it; at the same time the traditional
teaching on the Mass, briefly described above, has by and large
been adhered to, perhaps less in the intellectual sphere than in
the subjective formation of devotion. It is the same as putting
old wine into new vessels and nothing more. The substance

102

of the Eucharistic celebration is not explained to them, although it is only as an expression of this that the liturgy can be understood. There has been a demand for celebrating the Mass liturgically, but none of the same effort has gone to the catechetical exposition of the substance of the Eucharistic celebration, as it is now understood in the light of the liturgy. Here the second step has been taken before the first. To learn an expression by heart without giving sufficient attention to whether what is being expressed has been adequately understood, must necessarily lead to trouble. The feeling of something being out-of-place creeps in. It is to a large extent from these sources that the difficulties seem to arise regarding the introduction of children to a liturgical co-celebration of the Holy Sacrifice of the Mass.

Here, therefore, a basic reform of our catechetics on the Eucharist is indicated as the first requirement for the Children's Mass, as the situation is at present, and it should start with instruction in very early childhood, even before school-age. In the religious sphere the first impressions are precisely those which are decisive for children. It is at this point that the pastoral care of children and that of adults come most closely into contact. If a mother, in her spiritual life, has grasped even partially the substance of the Eucharistic celebration underlying the liturgical form, she will be able without difficulty to help her child in his first approach to the Eucharistic mystery. (For the most part this will be directed initially towards the reception of the Eucharistic bread.) Moreover, she will be able to impart this knowledge so that later on the child can understand the act of Eucharistic Sacrifice and thus join in the celebration liturgically though in a child's way. It would be beyond the scope of this

103

article to describe in more detail the fundamental lines of a teaching concerning the Eucharist for children in the spirit of the liturgical revival. The mere comment must suffice, that such teaching is the basis, as far as children are concerned, of all instruction in the real co-offering of the Mass. It is because so much has been lacking in this teaching in the past that we constantly come up against difficulties here, in spite of all efforts for the liturgical development of the Children's Mass.

Let us not exaggerate. There is no fundamental conflict between a joint-celebration of the Mass which is liturgical and one which is suited to the child. Provided they get the right teaching on the Eucharist at the same time, children are very easily introduced gradually, step by step, to the liturgical form of joint-celebration. Naturally this introduction has to take place step by step – and this refers as much to the teaching as to the joint-celebration itself.

What does all this involve for the children's joint-celebration at the Eucharistic Sacrifice?

1. Their joint-celebration must always be a real participation, that is, they must really be included and feel themselves included in the events of the Sacrifice of the Mass. For this reason a completely independent concurrent set of "devotions for children" should be avoided. The unity between the celebrant and the children must be preserved, at all costs, by the acclamations and responses of the community.

2. The official liturgical texts of the Mass can be replaced throughout by texts more suitable for children, where this seems to be necessary. In doing this care should, however, be taken to see that there is no prayer in the children's Mass which has nothing to do with the part of the Mass to which it corresponds.

The same holds good of the choice of hymns. It does not do to arouse faith, hope and charity at the Offertory, for instance, or sing a hymn to Our Lady at the Sanctus.

Here then there is scope for the gradual development of the children's participation. It is not necessary that all the liturgical thought and substance of the Eucharistic celebration should be expressed at every Mass. There is no doubt that at different age-levels children have a certain sympathy for certain aspects of Eucharistic worship. There seems to be no reason why this factor should not be the criterion in the selection of texts for the Children's Mass, as long as this choice only operates within the sphere of the profound mystery of the Eucharist and its liturgical worship. It is, for example, conceivable that with younger children it is more the idea of the Mass as a communal meal which is expressed, with the older ones more its sacrificial character. Similarly the Mass as *"Eucharistia"* and as *"Memoria"* could serve as the main underlying idea for the prayers of a Children's Mass, as might one of the major concerns of the Universal Church or the basic motive of the liturgical cycle. For the little ones even a shortening of the individual parts of the Mass itself seems to us possible and advisable, as long as the basic structure of the proceedings is left visible: preparation of the gifts, offering and meal. The ultimate aim is the adult Christian who has made the official liturgical form of the Eucharist his own so that he really is a co-celebrant with the priest.

3. Activity is part of the child's world, as is movement and visual presentation. Therefore everything which contributes to this should be brought into play in the Children's Mass: the standing, kneeling and sitting which has such significance, the Offertory Procession, the Communion procession, the solemn

entry of the priest and attendants, the dignified enactment of the duties of the servers, the responses, the alternation between reader, leader, and people, the contrast between spoken prayer and silence. The proper starting-point for all explanations is not the outer form but the inner meaning. The danger of lifeless functions, of an uncomprehended activity, becomes reality too easily; then a genuine approach and a real joy in the liturgical act are achieved only with difficulty. We have plenty of time and should not seize all the opportunities for liturgical formation all at once. Too often the second and third steps are made before the first.

4. The child should "grow" into the ordinary parish Sunday Mass. For this reason it is not a good thing for children to have their own type of Mass, even if it is modelled on the best liturgical lines, as is the case in Germany. High Mass and the Community Mass with the official liturgical texts should be offered by the children at the same time as and with the adults. Then, for the first time, they experience the full communion of the parish and also more easily avoid the danger of children's Masses and school Masses: that after the childhood stage Mass will be entirely neglected. Where special Children's Masses on Sundays are regularly necessary, the fixed and variable parts of the Mass should not be replaced by texts specially for children, although the Credo might be replaced by the Apostles' Creed and over-long and difficult Epistles and Gospels shortened. Any Sunday Mass, however, must always be a Mass suitable for the whole parish. It is precisely this gradual initiation of the children into the Sunday parish Mass which has caused the French Catholic Directory to regard Children's Masses on Sundays as a "far from ideal solution". (No. 242; cp. also Nos. 232, 241 ff.)

106

9

The Vigil as an Evening Service for the Parish

JOSEPH GELINEAU

THE word "vigil" is not used here in its etymological sense of a night watch, neither is it used in the sense of the rubrics as the preparation for a feast nor in that of previous liturgical practice (as today in the restored Easter Vigil), but in the wider sense of a specifically Christian type of service which unites in itself the essential elements of our worship.

J. A. Jungmann has evolved the following basic elements of Christian worship: Reading, Hymn and Prayer, the last being divided into People's Prayer and Priest's Prayer. Jungmann has demonstrated that these elements are component parts of every truly liturgical action and, basing himself on the liturgical books, has described the characteristic features of these fundamental liturgical elements. They are found at their purest and simplest in the structure of the Vigil.

The Vigil may be regarded as one of the two basic forms of Christian worship. The first and principal one is the celebration of the Eucharist which has as its "sign" the Lord's Supper and which is re-enacted by the Church according to the Lord's command: "Do this for a commemoration of me" (1 Cor. 11:24–25). The celebration of the Eucharist is preceded by a service of the Word, the "sign" of which is the proclamation of the glad tidings according to the Lord's command: "Go ye

107

and teach all nations" (Matt. 28:19). The proclaiming of the faith is to effect the conversion and then lead to baptism by means of continuing instruction. But the act of proclaiming must also be carried on for those who have already been initiated into the mysteries. It is never at an end even after baptism, for it is the duty of the baptized person constantly to scrutinize his position of *Metanoia*: "a man must examine himself first and then eat of this bread and drink of that cup" (1 Cor. 11:28). And he can only pass such a judgment on himself by constantly facing up to the commands of the New Covenant: "The man who loves me is the man who keeps the commandments he has from me" (John 14:21). Therefore the Mass, as the proper Christian worship, consists of the double rite of Scripture and Meal, a rite which every time puts before us a twofold table: that of the "word" of life and that of the "bread" of life.

Not only does the Church never celebrate the Eucharist unless it is preceded by the preaching of the Gospel (the Sacrament translates into reality what Scripture reveals), but she goes on extending her pre-Eucharistic catechetical function. At the time when the catechumens were still in a separate category, aliturgical synaxes were arranged at certain intervals in Lent. These were meetings for worship without the celebration of the Eucharist, at which the *Photizomenoi* were instructed and those already "initiated" perfected. The Vigils of Feasts (particularly the Easter Vigil) served as occasions for a revision of the instruction and a more intensive time of prayer. The development of the catechism from the Counter-Reformation onwards and of the missions to ordinary people, even though these are less in the traditional form than the Vigil, springs from the same concern.

108

The Hours of communal prayer in the morning or evening whether in the monastic or parochial sphere, have their origin in a form related to the Vigil.

In short, the demand for more intensive instruction or the fervour of the communities presuppose other meetings separate from the Mass. The Vigil is a traditional answer to this twofold need.

Of what does a Vigil consist? We still have a living model in the Easter Vigil or in the aliturgical synaxis of Good Friday or (even though truncated) in the first part of the Mass. In all these we see clearly the component elements and their arrangement. On Easter Night we find the sequence:

(a) Reading from the Scriptures
(b) Singing of a biblical Canticle
(c) People's Prayer (silent, after "*Oremus. Flectamus genua*")
(d) Priest's Prayer, summing up (*Collecta*).

This sequence is repeated as often as is necessary – four times at present. The Good Friday service, of which the basic elements go back to the fourth century, is constructed in the same way. The outline is repeated quite simply after each of the three Readings. The Solemn Prayers of Intercession at the end unite the whole:

(a) Reading from Osee
(b) Canticle of Habacuc
(c) Silent Prayer of the People
(d) Priest's *Collecta*
(a) Reading from Exodus
(b) Psalm 139
(a) The Passion according to St. John

109

(c)–(d) The Solemn Intercessions which unite the People's Prayer and the Priest's Prayer.

The first part of the Mass has basically the same construction. Apart from the opening rite, which goes as far as the Collect inclusive and is, as it were, a vestibule which was added to the main building later, since Augustine began immediately with the Readings, we have:

(a) Epistle
(b) Gradual – responsorial psalm
(a) Gospel
(c)–(d) *Oratio fidelium* (intercessions)

This last element, preceding the Offertory, unfortunately disappeared from the Roman Mass at the end of the fifth century.

The traditional part which has remained unchanged is therefore:

(a) Reading from the Scriptures
(b) Singing of a Psalm or biblical Canticle
(c) People's Prayer (intercessory or silent)
(d) Priest's Prayer, summing up.

This sequence is in no way arbitrary. It corresponds to the Christian pattern of salvation.

(1) Every Church ceremony opens with the proclamation of the message of Revelation. For only God can begin our salvation and show us the way to his kingdom.

(2) The whole congregation give their assent to this proclamation by a united confession of faith. The natural expression

110

of this is in song. In general, this song is a psalm or a biblical canticle in responsorial form. (The reason for this will be seen later.)

(3) But the congregation knows that the work of salvation is not yet finished. It must pray for the Church which is still on its journey. It must pray for its leaders, for its sinful members, for those who are not yet re-united with the flock.

(4) And this prayer finds its fulfilment in the prayer of the head of the parish who represents the High Priest. He collects together *(Collecta)* the intentions of the prayers of the community in a set form so that the prayer of the Church reaches the Father through the Son in the Holy Ghost.

Before embarking upon the study of the Vigil ceremony by analyzing its elements, we must consider the pastoral interest of such a service.

This type of service disappeared all too soon from the history of the Western Liturgy. When the special status of catechumens was dropped, the Lenten aliturgical synaxes fell into disuse. The daily prayer of the monastic communities found a new form in the Canonical Hours of the present Roman Office. Our parishes hold traditional devotions on Sundays and certain other days, which are perfectly suitable for the people's prayer and occasionally Vespers or Compline are sung too. Apart from the fact that the Easter Vigil has been re-instituted, in what respect can the Vigil concern us?

We might consider whether the deepest needs of the Christian people are being fulfilled as things stand at present and whether the liturgical revival, which has made a special attempt to present the Mass ceremonies more perfectly, would not bear some fruit also in this connection.

The re-institution of the Easter Vigil demands the re-introduction of preparation for the Easter mysteries: of Lent as a special time of instruction and prayer. A Lenten sermon gains a quite different value if it is not just an isolated sermon, (even though surrounded by hymns and prayers) but fitted organically into a liturgical frame. It can only ever be possible for a few to attend the daily Masses in Lent (since most are prevented by the demands of their work) but participation in some Vigils as a preparation for Easter could command a wider public.

Some types of popular devotion do, of course, have a high pastoral value and contain in their basic form the essential elements of Christian worship: passages from the Scriptures, hymns, antiphonal prayers, priest's prayers. It is, however, true that they do not always present these elements in the liturgically traditional form and that, for this reason, they lose certain valuable features to which our age would be particularly responsive: the importance given to Scripture, the singing of the psalms, the communal intercessions, the set form of the ceremony.

The fact that many devotions have been replaced by Vespers and Compline in their liturgical form may be regarded an advance. Though indisputable as such, this development poses nonetheless a question as regards liturgical pastoral care. In the first place let us make clear that the real traditional evening prayer is not Compline, so popular today, but Vespers. But both Offices – like the other Hours too – have received from the monastic setting in which they developed a form which is more suited to a monastic community than a parish. The singing of a large number of psalms by alternating choirs is not deeply rooted in the ordinary prayer of the faithful. On the contrary, the present service shows a curtailing of Bible reading and of intercessory prayer for the needs of the Church – both of which are of the greatest value for our people. The structure and content of the Vigil are more suitable for communal prayer than the canonical or monastic Hours, as we have them today as the outcome of an historical development.

Finally some observers claim that a Sunday evening service does not fit very well into the rhythm of modern life, particularly in the towns, and that those who attend these services are not always very animated. Suggestions have been made that a new importance should once again be given to the evening service on Saturday, as a preparation for Sunday Mass,[1] and this ceremony would basically be a Vigil. If this happened, there would be an opportunity to return once again to the original structure of this service. At the beginning it would be held at least on the evening before great feasts and also on certain Sundays in Advent and Lent.

How then are the different elements of a Vigil actually to be transformed into reality?

1. Reading from the Bible and Homily

The Bible should not seem to be merely an excuse for a sermon or a starting-point for meditation. It is the solemn proclamation of the word of salvation. It should be read or sung from the *ambo* or pulpit in the choir by a reader in liturgical dress facing the congregation and from a book the very appearance of which arouses reverence. The reader fetches the book from

[1] In the hope that it might be possible to end the Saturday evening Vigil with the celebration of the Eucharist, which would then be the Sunday Mass.

the altar and, accompanied by two acolytes, bears it in procession to the *ambo* (he could also ask for the priest's blessing). It would be wrong to read the word of God from the nave; for it does not come from the community, but is rather addressed to it and it is proper that all should listen to it rather than that each should read for himself.

There are two schools of thought which can guide us as far as the choice of reading is concerned. The oldest is that of the *lectio continua*. A book is chosen from Holy Scripture and a passage from it read at each Vigil. In the final homily the whole book could be explained to the congregation, an excellent means of "proclaiming the word" and of Bible instruction. During Advent, for example, Isaiah could be read; after the Epiphany or Pentecost one of the four Evangelists. In this way one parish-priest explained the Apocalypse daily during the Month of our Lady.

The second is one where the choice takes into account the liturgical feast which is being celebrated or prepared for or else is in harmony with the liturgical season. During Lent the epistles from the daily Masses could be used, an excellent preparation for the baptismal symbolism of Easter Eve.

An explanation must follow every reading from the Scriptures. "Proclamation of the word" includes both the Bible as basis and the sermon which makes it penetrate the life and faith of the people. Traditionally, this sermon is a homily which follows the reading closely point by point and explains it in its literal as well as its spiritual sense. In this way it contributes to the value of the Vigil as a means of Christian education. If no priest is present, the homily could occasionally be replaced by a reading from the Fathers or a passage from a sacred author.

114

2. Responsorial Singing of a Psalm

The assembled congregation respond to the word of God with a song. Singing is the ideal form of expression for a parish. According to tradition, however, we give our answer to God in his own words. Not just any and every composition is suitable; it must be a psalm or biblical canticle, for the psalms are the poetic expression of the whole Bible and the perfect summary of the Christian mysteries. The psalm should be chosen in the context of the reading and should form a continuation of it.[1]

By tradition this psalm is still chanted in responsorial form: a reader-cantor chants the psalm from the ambo (not from the choir-stalls) to a simple melody and all answer with a short "response" inserted in between all the verses (or rather groups of verses)[2]. The significance of this arrangement must be understood for it is neither one of pure chance nor simply of practical convenience; a mystery is embodied in it. The psalm is also the word of God: it is to be taken up by the Church through her servant who declaims it. But it must also be returned to him by all present and answered with an unanimous cry: "Lord, have mercy upon us", "Alleluia", and so on. Thus there develops a dialogue between God and his people, the conversation of bridegroom and bride. Experience shows that this form of psalmody, which has the oldest tradition in the

---

[1] Such was the custom at the ceremonies in the synagogue and this explains the titles of many psalms, which connected them with the episodes in the historical books after which they came. In the old psalters the psalms also had appropriate headings which related them to the Christian mysteries.

[2] Originally the chants of the Easter Vigil had this responsorial form.

Christian liturgy (the responsorial psalm after the reading) is also the most contemplative. It would be a good idea for the homily to expound the chief verse of the psalm and the text of the response. From a practical point of view, this form permits a different psalm to be chosen at each Vigil, for the response can be taken up immediately by everyone, if the reader-cantor has sung it once or twice.

3. The People's Petitions

The third element, too, has its roots in the solid and universal tradition of the Church. All churches have prayed for the great general intentions in obedience to the Apostle's admonition: "I desire, therefore, first of all, that supplications, prayers, inter-cessions and thanksgivings be made for all men, for kings and for all that are in high station, that we may lead a quiet and a peaceable life in all piety and chastity" (1 Tim. 2:1f). Prayers of petition which are admirable examples have thus been created: the *Orationes sollemnes* of Good Friday (probably the old *Oratio fidelium* of the Roman Mass), the *Deprecatio Gelasii,* the old Milanese litanies, and the Stowe Missal *(Divinae pacis* and *Dicamus omnes)* and the innumerable litanies of the deacons in the Eastern liturgy. Translated literally they are of surprising topicality. In them we pray for the whole Church and the peace of the world; for the heads of the Church: Pope, bishops, priests; for all degrees of people: virgins, married, children; for the secular authority and the rulers of the state; for all those suffering, ill, in prison or persecuted; for those not present, for our separated brethren; for the Jews and the infidels; for the dead. Usually the deacon states the intention: "For the Holy

Church of God: that our God and Lord would be pleased to give it peace, maintain it in union, and preserve it over the earth." – to which all answer: "Kyrie eleison" – "Lord, have mercy upon us."

After these general and timeless intentions it is permissible to choose some more specific and up-to-date ones. For the faithful this moment is one of the most moving of the Vigil: after the proclamation and the acceptance of God's word come the intercessions. The word received from God goes back to him in prayer. After the litany there might well be a time for silent prayer when everyone can offer up his own intentions privately and then the Vigil ends with the Lord's Prayer, the Our Father.

4. The Priest's Prayer

It is the priest's responsibility to end the prayer by summing up with a formula which outlines the main intentions (in the context of the reading or the Liturgical Year) in a *Collecta* addressed to the Father through the Son in the Holy Spirit, which is confirmed by the Amen of all those present. A liturgical Collect may be used or another prayer may be composed.

Because of its great simplicity the basic pattern of the Vigil is highly adaptable and can be used on very different occasions. It fits equally well into an ordinary parish service as into short family or guild evening prayers or the ceremonies at a large pilgrimage or congress. It may be cut down to a few minutes or made to last several hours according to the weight given to each of the separate parts. In particular, one can have several readings, each followed by a meditative psalm and also by a time for silent prayer and an *Oratio* as on Easter Eve. Intercessions and the final *Oratio* should, however, be reserved for the final sequence. The ceremony can begin with the solemn entry of the sacred ministers in procession accompanied by a hymn or by Ps. 94. It may be combined with the Sacramental Blessing (exposition starting at the beginning of the prayer section) so that the service closes with the *Tantum Ergo* and the Blessing, followed perhaps with a hymn to Our Lady.

In several countries this tradition of the Vigil has been revived in many parishes. It would seem to be in harmony with the present liturgical and biblical revival in the Church, as well as with the desire of the people of our time for us to break the bread of God's word for them and with their need to pray for and with the whole Catholic Church.

10

The Schola

PAUL GUTFLEISCH

THE name *"schola"* is not found in liturgical books, where reference is generally made to "cantores" and "chorus". The liturgical chants are divided in hierarchical order in the following way: *celebrans, cantores, chorus* and *omnes* (as, for example, at the Veneration of the Cross on Good Friday according to the new order).

In the golden age of the liturgy and of Gregorian chant and up until the late Middle Ages, the cantors and the choir came from the *schola cantorum,* the choir-school which was attached to every important church. The choirs were always made up of boys *(pueri cantores)* and men; they wore liturgical clothing during the services and sat in the chancel, which thus eventually came to be called the choir.

During the fifteenth and sixteenth centuries this state of affairs began to change everywhere, perhaps as a result of the Reformation. The choir-schools ceased to exist; the *pueri cantores* diminished in numbers and were replaced by women's voices; the choir left the chancel, where it was no longer required, and took up its position in the choir loft at the back of the church. This last change indicated spatially also that the choir had taken on a different function from previously: it was now representing the people and singing their part, the Ordinary of the Mass. Admittedly, at that time compositions and performances were often of a high quality.

The liturgical revival of recent years makes firm demands for changes and restorations while avoiding any condemnation of worthwhile achievements: for instance, the utilizing of women's voices in church-choirs, which is certainly valuable in many respects.

The chants which really belong to the choir must no longer be neglected. These are the Proper of the Mass, (which was for centuries only whispered by the celebrant) and the antiphonal chants in the psalmodies of Vespers and Compline.

The people must be made once more to accept and adopt joyfully the chants which are proper to them: the Ordinary of the Mass, the psalms at Vespers, the acclamations.

New experiments create new duties, as, for example, in the German "Parish-Masses". The group of singers taking over these liturgical duties is appropriately called the *schola*. Since the schola is used on all Sundays and feast days at High Mass, it has to be a very flexible and willing group of singers, a liturgical diaconate. It would be desirable to try to form it from the men in the existing choir, since most churches have one. But if the church-choir should find the duties too alien to them, that is if they are unprepared spiritually or have vocal qualities which make them unsuitable, there will be no alternative but to approach other singers: these will usually be enthusiastic young people. Unfortunately, the church-choir will not always view this schola kindly; for this reason there should, where possible, be the same choir-master for both choirs so that there is at least some guarantee that gradually opposition will change to collaboration.

The liturgical chants, particularly the melismatic chants of the plainsong, should be sung without an organ accompaniment; they take their vitality entirely from the human voice. The importance of vocal training for the schola is thus obvious. Any screeching or bellowing and so forth would be an annoyance to the congregation and inexcusable; every choir-practice should begin with singing exercises.

The Gregorian chants should be sung with everyone sharing one large plainsong book; then all the singers can see the choir-master's signals and the singing will be unified in timing and rhythm.

If the schola sings the *Proprium choraliter* every Sunday, then two practices a week would seem essential the first year, later on half-an-hour to an hour will be sufficient.

The choir's position has to be decided by local conditions; fortunately the relationship of altar and choir has been observed in new church buildings.

Gregorian chant only really comes to life if it is possible to have upper and lower parts singing antiphonally. It is preferable to use women's voices rather than altogether to dispense with the upper voice ranges. It is without a doubt best of all to train boy-singers for the upper parts. This is a very demanding task. But anyone who has experienced the almost magical effect of boys' voices on a congregation and seen how it responds by joining joyfully in the singing, will gladly take the demanding task upon himself.

It is a pre-requisite of any rewarding work with choir-boys that the choir-master should be gifted as a teacher even more than he is as a musician and that he should be prepared also to devote some of his free time to the boys.

121

The boys usually require two hours of practice on two different days. The best thing is to recruit the group of "beginners" from the first-communicants for two practices of about 30 minutes. Altogether this makes three to four hours of choirwork with the boys. Who has this time to spare? Who has the love necessary for the work? Who will pay the choir-master?

In some places the vocal talent is scarce, and less than ten per cent of the boys who attend Sunday Mass are both suitable and reliable. Elsewhere more than fifty per cent volunteer and their potential talent should not be allowed to go to waste.

When the schola is sufficiently trained it should be given its proper place once again in the chancel and in liturgical dress. (For liturgical dress the black cassock and cotta or alb are recommended; eccentricities should be avoided.)

The regularity of routine, habit, the symptoms of fatigue of a spiritual sort, which the celebrant experiences himself, affects the schola too; for this reason the schola needs not just musical but pastoral care.

It is a surprising and encouraging experience that wherever the services are consistently and carefully arranged so that the schola is indispensable, there results a sense of responsibility and reliability among its members. Many of the boys may discover a vocation to the priesthood or to become church organists.

11

The Lector

FERDINAND KOLBE

WE have learnt to attach great importance once again to the readings from the Word of God within the Mass itself. This development must be accentuated further. We are thus justified in giving special attention to the office of lector. Let us hear first of all what the liturgical scholar has to say:

"Early in the Church's history a special reader was appointed for the performance of the readings – always someone other than the leader of the divine service, as we see already in Justin. There is a certain amount of drama in this; the word which comes from God is spoken by a different person than the word which rises from the church to God. Even if Justin does not actually present the office of lector, that office does certainly appear in the second century as a special position; the lector is the oldest of the lesser degrees of ordination. It is clear that the lector has to have, or to receive, a certain amount of education. But this was not the only thing kept in view in choosing him. It is a remarkable fact that since the fourth century in the West – especially in Rome – boys appear preponderantly as lectors."[1]

We can deduce three things from this. First of all, the great antiquity of the office of lector. For us the server belongs almost

[1] J. A. Jungmann: *The Mass of the Roman Rite,* Engl. transl. London 1958, p. 268.

as much to the Mass as the priest but the lector appears to be a rather arbitrary innovation and one with which we can dispense. History, however, teaches us that originally the lector was just as much a part of the Mass. Let us use this fact to arouse enthusiasm for the office of lector. But our reason for fostering his proper function is that through it the special importance of the preaching of the Word is emphasized. The aim ought to be to have a lector taking part in every Mass in which the people participate whether on Sundays or weekdays. Wherever there is a congregation, the Word of God must be proclaimed; where the Word is proclaimed, there ought to be a lector.

Secondly, we are given some indication of who should perform the office of lector. In recent years there has been a tendency in Germany to remove boys from this sacred function as much as possible. Quite apart from the practical difficulties this has caused, there is little historical basis for this tendency. And present-day experience confirms that sometimes boys from the age of thirteen onwards and before their voices break perform their task as lectors excellently. But this age-group is not always suitable. As far as the importance of the office is concerned it is preferable to choose adults or at least young men. This is especially true of special Masses for children, a rewarding task perhaps for the teachers. But a second priest, who is free to do it, should occasionally perform the office in order to stress the dignity of the Word of God. Of course, there is no question of using girls or women, and even at a special service for a girls' school the lector in the liturgical sense ought not to be dispensed with.

Finally it is said that the office of lector introduces a dramatic element into the divine service. We know well enough from experience that the inner value of the liturgy is not by itself sufficient to hold the attention of the congregation; other exterior elements must be added to counteract apathy. In this respect the function of the lector is indeed a very important one, especially as the celebrant carries out his duties with his back to the people. For this reason the lector should not also be the one to lead the prayers.

What then is the task of the lector at the different types of Mass?

At Solemn High Mass he is not used; deacon and subdeacon read both Epistle and Gospel, also in the vernacular.

At the ordinary Sung Mass, on the other hand, the lector reads the Epistle, the celebrant the Gospel.

At Low Mass, at any rate according to the practice of the German *Gemeinschaftsmesse* (Community-Mass), the lector proclaims both Epistle and Gospel.

But the order for High Mass can also be adopted by the celebrant's reading of the Latin texts up to and including the Gospel in a low voice, while the Epistle and Gradual are read aloud (as at High Mass), and then himself reading the Gospel in the vernacular. In this way there is the same gradation as at Sung Mass: the Epistle is read by the lector, the Gospel by the celebrant.

The reading aloud of any other lessons (but not of prayers) is also the concern of the lector. For example, he reads the Prophecies during the Easter Vigil.

In contrast to someone who may lead the prayers, the lector holds a liturgical office. Therefore he should wear liturgical dress (long black cassock and surplice or possibly an alb), which looks better than ordinary clothes. He ought not to use any book the appearance of which would not be in keeping with the dignity of the occasion.

He reads the texts from the front of the church facing the congregation. In churches of normal size (that is those in which one can be heard everywhere when speaking from the altar) he will stand in the choir, otherwise on the steps of the choir or in front of the benches. In places with bad acoustics it would be necessary to use a microphone, for intelligibility is the first rule. Churches should not be built in which one cannot make oneself heard from the choir without a loudspeaker.

The person appointed as lector must show himself worthy of this honourable position in his way of life and in his participation in the devotional life of the parish.

He must bring to his task an above-average intelligence, a good voice and a certain natural aptitude for reading aloud. It is a well-known fact that many priests do not possess these qualities and never learn to read aloud well. There is then even less reason for appointing someone as lector without first making sure of his aptitude for it. But talent alone is not sufficient; instruction and practice are necessary additions.

The lector must know when he has to go to the place from which the readings are to be given, so that he does not disturb the rest of the liturgy, such as the silent prayer after the Oremus. (It is both sensible and practical for him to have his seat in the choir throughout the service so that he does not need to make a "big entrance".) He must know when to begin. (He may give the title of the Epistle immediately after the congregation's Amen to the Collect and then wait until the congregation is seated; or else the congregation sits down first and he then begins the reading with the title address.) He must know the

126

headings of the Epistles (not all missals have this in the vernacular). He must know the correct pronunciation of any unusual names which occur.

The lector must adjust his voice to the size of the church. His reading must be slow enough for everyone to take in the meaning easily (above all a definite pause should be made at the end of every sentence); and yet vivid enough to hold the attention. There is no need for a monotonous voice; he should speak in a natural way, appropriate to the meaning.

Any inaccuracies of pronunciation should be corrected, also the swallowing of individual syllables or even of individual letters. A tape-recorder can be useful for practice. We ought to practise careful speech not only for the sake of intelligibility but because of the dignity of the Word of God. Here, certainly, the celebrant must lead the way by his good example.

It is advisable and urgent that, beyond the parish, the diocese should make the instruction of lectors its concern.

To sum up, the office of lector, which is venerable by its great antiquity, merits every care and encouragement. In contrast with the leader, the lector has a positive liturgical function. In contrast with the server, he has an important spiritual task. He gives his service to the word, ill-served as it often is in holy places; he serves the Word of God. A good deal of the vital and dignified form of divine services depends on him.

12

The Church Choir

Alfons Kirchgaessner

A parish without a church choir is indeed poor; on feast-days it is deprived of all lustre. But a parish with a church choir that has not understood what it is and what it ought to be is yet poorer. The church choir is not a Catholic singing group using the divine office as an occasion for inflicting its performances on us; nor is it a society for the improvement of local amenities, whose main task it would be to brighten up the services with "extras". Like the *schola,* the church choir is one of the pillars of the liturgical action.

In support we can quote from the *Motu proprio* of Pius X, "*Tra le sollecitudini*" of 1903: "The musica sacra is an essential component of the solemn liturgy" and "In the Church singers occupy a liturgical office in the true sense." Where the leader of the choir is a conductor who is deeply conscious of this fact, the choir will be protected, at least in the long run, from giving itself airs or feeling professional jealousy towards an existing or developing *schola.*

An important distinction between *schola* and choir must certainly be pointed out: whereas the schola is completely tied to the liturgy, the church choir both can and should, according to its ability, give concerts too, either at evenings devoted to sacred music or at parish functions outside the immediate liturgical sphere.

128

The chief trouble is the liturgical education and outlook, or lack of it, of the choir-master. If his own formation proves inadequate, he ought to make up for it by study courses or at least by discussion with the parish-priest and by special reading. It is a joy to have a "cantor" – this old and venerable title might perhaps be re-introduced in time – with whom there are no differences of opinion on questions of liturgical correctness, for the simple reason that he has sufficient knowledge of what the liturgy is and what the musician owes it.

Such a conductor will allow the members of the choir increasingly to share his own knowledge by his occasional comments or short talks, so that the point is reached when everyone gives of his best from a spiritual joy in the liturgy and not just from pleasure in the music.

Every parish-priest should remind himself from time to time of the sacrifices the singers make and he should always have a word of appreciation for them to help maintain the enthusiasm without which a choir cannot continue. Under no circumstances should he express his disapproval, except when this is warranted by their conduct during services, by intrigues or a lack of charity among the members. He should find time, too, to spend an occasional social hour with his choir – perhaps on St. Cecilia's Day!

No-one would expect the priest to come to every choir-practice, yet on the other hand everyone would feel annoyed if he never put in an appearance at a rehearsal the whole year round. These visits to the choir either at regular intervals or before feast-days are good opportunities for a few quick words of advice, which may increase the understanding of the Liturgical Year, the sacred words or of the structure of the Mass. It is not advisable to speak at length on these occasions, as this would hinder the work of the practice.

Apart from this, the aim should be for all the singers to take part in days of recollection; the ideal is to have special days for church musicians and singers. In dioceses where such days are not arranged, it should not be difficult to organize a special parish day of recollection once every few years. In some places in Germany and France "Church Music Study Weeks" have been organized which combine practical studies with theoretical and spiritual instruction and which, above all, allow the musicians to take part in model services; the importance of sacred music makes a further extension of such arrangements seem highly advisable. Wherever they were started, good results were seen to follow. Even if not all the members of the choir can take part, those who do will become a "leaven" amongst the others.

In most of our churches with their galleries, the distance spatially between the choir and the altar is unfortunately great and is a major obstacle in the way of the choir's participation in the Eucharistic meal. Here ways and means must be found of overcoming the existing difficulties. It should not be a matter of indifference to the priest whether his organist and choir-master go weekly to Communion or perhaps only once at Easter or thereabouts; nor whether the members of the choir take part actively in the sacramental life of the Church or whether precisely when they do distinguish themselves actively – as they do, above all, on feast-days – they cut themselves off from the participation at the Lord's table. Admittedly, one must act with circumspection here to avoid any unpleasant feeling of control or moral obligation; but a feeling for the real merit of active participation must be awakened and fostered.

130

In Germany new opportunities for the collaboration of the choir at services have been provided by new hymn-books: for example, antiphonal singing with the congregation, which enables the rich repertoire of polyphonic music to be added to the best hymns; and responsorial singing, which also offers the opportunity for a polyphonic psalmody "faux bourdon". This means that the church-choir could and should collaborate not only at High Mass but also at Low or dialogue Masses and at devotions.

Naturally the choir has an important job in learning and rehearsing new hymns as well as new Plainsong Masses. It may accompany the cantor or priest while he is not yet perfect – which is far better than having the organ play the tune through first. Above all, it can back up the still timid singing of the congregation, at best "posted" in their midst. At Plainsong Masses when the schola usually takes over the Proper and the singing of the Ordinary the choir should be at hand, instead of taking up the old superficial attitude: "It's the schola's turn today, not ours." A choir which regards it as its honour and duty to serve the singing congregation quite unobtrusively in this way, gives the best possible account of itself.

This can, however, only happen when the choir is educated liturgically and this remains a permanent task for the responsible priest.

13

The Organist

ALFONS KIRCHGAESSNER

THE value of an organist is recognized for the first time, when one day an inadequate substitute has to take his place. How unfortunate the parish which has grown so accustomed to the incompetence of its organist that it experiences something of pleasing shock when someone else takes the accustomed seat at the instrument. Since the organ's voice rules the whole place regally, it is quite incomprehensible why so many priests everywhere have so little concern for the person who "calls the tune"; and not only for his abilities as a performer but also for his religious attitude, which inevitably shows itself in his playing, and for his liturgical education, the deficiencies of which must lead to constant disagreement.

Naturally there can be no very detailed discussion here of the education of our full or part-time organists. Here we can discuss only the fundamental attitude which is essential and towards which every parish-priest should guide the servant of the musica sacra, even when the priest knows little about music – for this, unfortunately, is often an excuse for letting the organist have a free hand.

It could be said of the organist at Mass (as it is of the divine wisdom) that he "plays before God". The house of God is neither a concert-hall nor a rehearsal-room: here everything should

132

redound to the praise of God and to the edification of the faithful. For this reason the musician should give of his best with a devout heart. His way of active participation is his playing and thus he should open the lid of his organ with the same feelings with which another man opens his prayerbook. Consequently the priest should respect his organist as collaborator and associate in the formation of the divine office and not regard him as an underling whose only duty it is, as it were, to let some fresh air into a musty atmosphere.

An important difference between the Protestant and the Catholic organist is the greater scope given the former whose playing often is almost the focal point of the ceremony, whereas the latter rarely has any opportunity for greater performances and basically has a purely serving function. He may never at any point keep the priest waiting, never hold up the flow of the liturgical action. The opportunity to play classical music comes only after Mass, if we except the greater possibilities of a solemn High Mass or those of a lengthy distribution of Communion. His playing within the Mass must be quite brief and take its form from the context: his introductions should indicate melody and tempo exactly, particularly for the lesser known hymns, and must, in any case, keep within strict limits. These circumstances are chiefly to blame for the fact that the art of improvisation is but little developed among most of our organists and yet the limited form demands a greater degree of skill in improvisation since it gives the organist far less time to develop a theme. Much of what we have to listen to between hymns has, in fact, nothing to do with art and is purely the result of this dilemma. It has been well described as "doodling on the keys".

How seriously an organist takes his position can be judged by whether he prepares his services in advance. This preparation is threefold: firstly, the appropriate choice of hymns which have some relation both to the course of the action and the text of the Proper; secondly, the study of classical pieces (pride alone should keep any moderately competent musician from playing, year in year out, whatever happens to come into his head); thirdly, the practising of small improvisations above a cantus firmus. Ability to improvise may be a gift, but a great deal can be achieved by diligent practice.

It is difficult to understand why the organist should give priests their lead. It can be quite embarrassing when this is not taken up because the priest's hearing is defective or because he just doesn't feel like it. Again, why should the organist accompany the responses? An Amen is no more lively nor more festive on account of the organ's intervention. Since we reject the peculiar habit of playing the accompaniment to the priest, we might also desist from the custom of providing mere background music all the time for the congregation's singing. Moreover both the organist's devotion and his playing might benefit if not every silence were filled in by a few bars on the organ. What matters is that the organist should adapt his playing to the style of a hymn or choral work. He will improvise differently for a plainsong Mass (above all not softly and romantically nor playfully in the baroque manner) than for a Mozart Mass unless he prefers in the latter case not to improvise at all). He will also endeavour, stylistically and in his choice of stops, to convey some feeling for the musical and textual individuality of a hymn: he will treat the introduction as well the accompaniment quite differently in "Faith of our fathers," "To Jesus' Heart all-burning" and "O purest of creatures". Monotony

134

of phrasing and of choice of register often appears to be lack of warmth or indifference. It would be claiming too much to say that the organist should preach through his instrument, but it is not too much to ask that he should interpret the sacred music and help the people to sing it with heart and soul.

Like a choir which aspires to be rather better than average, a talented organist should find opportunities to show his ability outside the liturgy in services of sacred music or church concerts. Here some compensation at least can be found for the customary irreverence with which the congregation, as it streams out after Mass, literally tramples upon a Bach Fugue or a Prelude by some old or modern composer. The fact that relatively few people attend evening events of this kind will and should not deter those who enjoy music from working systematically for the education of the people of the parish; they must, however, feel sure that they have the active and heartfelt support of the parish-priest in their efforts. Only when we, as members of the Church, give them the honour and attention which is rightfully their due, can we eventually reach a general standard among our organists comparable to that among Protestant church musicians.

In conclusion, a few pen portraits, of a negative sort, of organists we have met. They are not intended to help us recognize in them the organist of our own parish, but to indicate the direction in which priests might exert themselves in securing the right kind of support from their organist.

There is the "routine" type who can do everything, has everything under control, needs no preparation and no forethought, never worries about anything nor exerts himself. Why should he?

135

There is the talkative type who chats to someone in every free moment he has or else flicks over pages or reads (particularly during the sermon!). Even his playing is more like idle prattle than prayer.

The "organ-tamer" demands attention and admiration (just listen how well I play the pedals, how I can manage three manuals at the same time!); he has no regard for the course of the Mass, which serves him merely as an opportunity to show off; he cannot adapt himself to any style. Most of all he enjoys playing fortissimo or producing surprise effects.

The "conventionalist" bores to death even the most indulgent with his stereotyped phrases (especially his final cadenzas, resolved sevenths, and so on); he always selects exactly the same tempo and uses exactly the same stops.

The "savage" knows of no discipline either in tempo or harmony (he switches at whim from two parts to five- or six-part playing), or in key (his abrupt modulations are generally irrelevant to the music itself or even to the course of the service) or in style (sharp dissonances alternate with soupy harmonies, the beginnings of contrapuntal composition break off without reason).

There is the man of haste who usually arrives too late, whose playing has a breathless quality about it; he pounces on the congregation with a sudden introduction and never allows a single moment of peace and quiet.

The "bungler" makes incessant mistakes without a qualm; he never allows himself to be affected by criticism to the extent of practising with a view to improvement; because he sits enthroned above the heads of the others he considers himself already one of the elect.

136

No pastor should let young talent escape him, nor should he begrudge the costs which may be necessary, to ensure that servants worthy of the "queen of instruments" may train and develop and become true servants of the sacred liturgy.

14

Serving at the Altar

JOSEF KÖNIG

ALTAR-SERVERS are not a necessary evil, which one cannot do without simply because they facilitate the performance of the liturgy with their effortless skill or because they also contribute to its embellishment by their presence. Altar-servers are active participants in the sacred function. They have a definite and specialized part in the liturgy.

In the encyclical *Mediator Dei* and in *Ordo hebdomadae sanctae instauratus* the altar-servers' special status is given prominence. The standards according to which altar-servers are to be chosen and trained can be deduced from their liturgical function and the dignity connected with it.

1. Selection and Grading

The right selection and a worthy training, appropriate to the office of altar-server, will ensure the parish-priest not only a hand-picked group of servers but also a group of co-workers for the Kingdom of God outside the liturgical sphere. The most suitable time for choosing new altar-servers is, without a doubt, the time soon after the first Communion. Boys who have not yet received the Sacrament of the Altar should not be admitted to service in the sanctuary, since they are not able really to join

138

in the celebration until they are "complete" Christians. The selection is the concern of the priest in charge of the servers. There is now a general tendency to let boys continue as altar-servers after the age of fourteen. The view that it is a man's job is in keeping with the dignity and importance of the liturgy and also with the tradition of the Church.

From these points of view at any rate, some grading among altar-servers is necessary. Their education should be a reverent initiation into the sacred actions. Every new outward act that they learn must be brought to life by the explanation given of it and they should become familiar with the duty by having to perform it for a certain time. For this reason the training should not be precipitated. A slow process of introduction to the sacred functions corresponds to the laws of the young person's organic growth and to his powers of comprehension. The gradual introduction to the functions is moreover an excellent safeguard against early defections. Four grades were suggested by the German body in Düsseldorf concerned with the education of altar-servers:

1. *Torch-bearer:* server at evening devotions, burials, baptisms, and torch-bearer in more solemn ceremonies;
2. *Acolyte:* service at Holy Mass, thurifer at devotions;
3. *Thurifer:* acolyte at High Mass and thurifer at High Mass;
4. *Reader:* master of ceremonies, reader and leader.

2. Instruction for Altar-Servers

The dignity of their duties will have to be emphasized repeatedly to the young people selected and their behaviour frequently corrected. In their further training, as in their selection, a reasonable

139

discipline will prove advantageous. The altar Guild should not degenerate into a sort of approved school for problem children, but should form an elite from whom a high standard can be expected.

The training of the altar-servers takes place for the most part during special lessons. For boys these lessons are best given weekly, for young men monthly and for the men four times a year. There are plenty of obvious aids to help one in devising lessons for the boys. So here we shall only give a few suggestions as to the form of an hour's instruction for the men.

The skeleton plan of this instruction for the young and older men might be as follows:

Reading from the Scriptures – discussion of the reading – discussion of the duty rota – final prayer.

What topics could be treated? The following are examples:

1. The meaning of the liturgical duties and actions (genuflections, bells, etc.)

2. The meaning of the vessels and instruments (candlesticks, candles, chalice, etc.)

3. The Liturgical Year – an actualization of the life of Christ. – The cycle of feasts and the feasts of the Liturgical Year in their theological content and meaning. – Feasts of the Liturgical Year and customs.

4. The Sacraments from a liturgical viewpoint (starting from the external action to explain the theological content).

5. Explanation of the Mass.

6. The spiritual life of the servers: How do I prepare for Mass? How do I pray at Mass? Personal side of their spiritual

life (prayer, confession, reading of the Scriptures) – the self-discipline of the servers.

7. Practices.

Many priests are frightened of holding practices. In anxious dreams they see themselves confronted by a gang of teenagers impossible to control. But it need not be like that. Each practice should have two parts: a theoretical one which explains what there is to do and why it has to be done in a certain way; and a practical part which puts into practice what has been discussed.

The course of the *explanation* might arise out of the following questions:

1. What do we have to prepare? (e. g. Palm Sunday procession)
2. What happens in this ceremony?
3. What is the meaning of the ceremony?
4. What is the significance of this feast in relation to the rest of the Liturgical Year?

Without explanations or any spiritual guidance these practice lessons can easily become a dull drill-routine. As regards the actual rehearsal, it is best to have everything carried out in full rather than just in bare outlines. Omissions may later lead to confusions and to undesirable "flops" during the actual service.

When are these rehearsals to be held? At least before every special kind of service such as Confirmation, Corpus Christi, the Good Friday and Easter liturgies. To dispense with rehearsals is to incur the risk of a far from edifying performance of the liturgy. The dignified, undisturbed and smooth running of ceremonies of a feast will always impress the congregation and radiate something of the solemnity and grandeur of the heavenly liturgy, of which after all man's earthly existence is a reflection. A grumpy priest who impatiently orders the servers about can hardly be said to reflect the person of Christ, whose representative he is at the altar.

3. The Servers' Duty Rota

Some of us may be familiar with quarrels among servers over their duties in the sanctuary. They would prefer the pleasant tasks and shun the less agreeable ones. A division of duties is therefore indispensable.

A rota for altar-servers should be drawn up before the instruction hour and then read to the boys and, if necessary, altered. At the end of the month a rota is produced for the next month. To plan ahead for a longer period is rarely feasible. We ought to try to instil an awareness of the vocation of being an altar-server. It is an honourable duty to serve the Lord; it is not a question of pleasing the curate or parish-priest.

4. Servers and Payment

If the priest selects his servers without regard to social position, then this call to the sacred functions is an honour for the boy and his family. His respect for the altar-service would certainly be marred if servers were to be remunerated. Payments for the performance of certain functions – even only small amounts – are certainly wrong. The server does not work for money.

142

But there may be a case for rewarding the server's devotion to his duties by an occasional small present, for example, on his birthday or at Christmas. An occasional group outing, too, may be popular and the costs could be borne by the parish or the servers' own funds. If presents are given they should have some connection with the altar-service or religious knowledge in general. But we might remember that such presents should give pleasure too, and have some relation to the boy's interests.

5. The Servers' Clothing

Sometimes an early defection from the altar-service may be connected with the unsuitability of the servers' vestments. The boys will naturally feel uncomfortable in something that looks more like a girl's skirt than anything else.

In Germany we have evolved four guiding principles regarding liturgical clothing:

1. The dignity of the altar and of the sacred actions require vestments for boys and men that should be beyond reproach.

2. The vestments should consist of a cassock reaching to the ankles and a cotta.

3. Colours should be confined to red and black.

4. All feminine touches such as unnecessary lace should be avoided and there should be no imitation of the clothing of deacons or subdeacons.

6. Servers and Schola

In the train of the liturgical revival *scholas* of boys or young men have been formed in many Continental parishes. They meet for regular practices to prepare for the coming services. Basically we distinguish between the functions of the servers at the altar, and the *schola's* service in the choir. Frequently, however, many of the choir-boys are also servers. This may lead to rivalries which must be avoided; both groups are necessary for a well-constructed service. The ideal solution would be to have two distinct bodies, but this will be possible in big parishes only. There may have to be a compromise, but it should be one which leaves both *schola* and servers ready for their tasks. The priest concerned for the efficiency of both groups will find a golden mean, impairing neither the performance of the liturgy nor the enthusiasm of the boys and young men for service in sanctuary or choir. Members of the *schola* might, for instance, be allowed to serve at the altar on special festive occasions when their service as singers is not required.

7. A Sacristy for Servers

The sacristy is the place for the necessary preparations for public worship and for keeping the liturgical vessels and vestment. But it is a place for spiritual as well as material preparation.

The question arises whether a separate sacristy should be provided for servers and choir-boys and, if so, what should be borne in mind regarding its equipment?

If space is available there should certainly be a special room for the servers and singers. It could also be used for rehearsals and instruction. There is the danger, of course, that the boys might be tempted into mischief and chatter, since they are not directly under supervision. For this reason it would be preferable if the servers' sacristy could be easily supervised from the priests' sacristy.

144

The servers' sacristy should not be a storage room for everything that is not being used at the moment. Outer disorder is scarcely likely to encourage an inner composure. Order and cleanliness are called for here as much as in the priests' sacristy. The cassocks and cottas, arranged according to size, should be kept in cupboards which can be locked. Every cassock and cotta has a size-tag, which it is best to sew to the inside of the collar. Each server knows "his" size. On special feasts the Master of Ceremonies or sacristan might lay out the necessary clothing beforehand. The vestments could be hung according to size on a large coat-rail.

In the servers' sacristy the thurifer prepares the coal for the thurible. A place to keep the thurible might be found outside the sacristy, where it can hang during a service when it is not in use. The processional cross stands by the door, the candlesticks for the acolytes are placed on a table and the candles for the torch-bearers in a rack. Everything should be placed so that it can easily be reached. There should also be room for a bench and kneeler with prayer-card for preparation for and thanksgiving after Mass.

8. Familiarity breeds Contempt

Anyone dealing all the time with things sacred runs the risk of inward indifference. The priest who celebrates the Holy Sacrifice every day has to make constant efforts for his action to remain truly spiritual and not to become mechanical. The servers, too, are exposed to this danger, and to an even greater extent, since they are young and immature. We must try to meet this danger in the right way. Here are some suggestions:

1. No server should have to serve more than one Mass. The priest himself knows how difficult it is to concentrate in second or third Masses.

2. The boys like helping with decoration and arrangement in the sacristy or at the altar. This assistance is certainly valuable and good; their love of serving may grow through such active help. If, however, this help is required too often, it may turn into a danger. Lack of reverence and concentration in church is often the result of young people's over-familiarity with sacred things.

3. Before every service the altar-servers should say a preparatory prayer. After this there should be silence. The procession is formed. Silence is by far the most respectful preparation for entering the House of God.

4. A brief act of recollection might be recommended, especially on great feast-days when the number of servers and choir-boys increases the danger of restlessness and chatter. This can take the form of a prayer or a short explanation of the sacred act about to take place.

The encyclical *Mediator Dei* refers to the possibility of vocations to the priesthood developing among the servers. The altar becomes the natural focus of life and experience for the boys. They can grow into a happy community and benefit from an atmosphere that is truly good and sacred. Here the ground is being prepared for God's call. The education of servers has the priesthood as its aim and as its foundation. The reverent enactment of the sacred rites by the priest can point the way for the boys.

15

Some Criteria for Preachers

Theo Gunkel

The preacher's task is both particularly onerous and rewarding. Here for consideration are four criteria against which we can measure and test our sermons. They are criteria which show the specific difficulties as well as the heartening aspects.

1. Message

The preacher is messenger. He has a message to deliver from someone. He is envoy and emissary. This is the first thing to be kept in mind: a sermon is neither lecture, nor instruction; it is not a means of communicating practical wisdom, a philosophy of life, one's own opinions. It is a message. And the important point in delivering this message is, on the one hand, that it should be faithfully rendered, that nothing should be suppressed or adulterated and, on the other hand, that it should be communicated so that others can hear it. What the others do with it, whether they receive it, draw any conclusions from it and act upon it, all this is no longer the messenger's concern. His concern must be to deliver the message faithfully, so that it is really heard.

The Christian sermon is a message, indeed it is the message of established facts, of past and future events. *Magnalia Dei:* a message of what God has done and a proclamation of what he will yet do, of what happened in the act of Creation and in the act of Redemption – and therefore the message of what God is like and who he is; it is the proclamation of the hidden Kingdom of God, which came to pass through Jesus, and the announcement of his manifest coming with the ultimate triumph of God's power at the Judgement and the Last Day; it is the handing on of Christ's message: "Do penance – for the Kingdom of heaven is at hand."

These are the ultimate glad tidings – the *basileia theou* like the hidden treasure and the pearl of great price; he who finds it, will joyfully give up everything for it. It is the message of the fulfilment of the finest and greatest longing of which man's soul is capable. But for man as he is and for the world in its present condition such a message is both terrifying and incredible. The message is concerned with a few important points, a few decisive facts. But what matters is to let it be seen from an infinite variety of viewpoints, to apply it to ever new situations, continually to open up new approaches.

The trouble is that the message is always greater than the messenger, the challenge is always greater than the messenger's fulfilment of it. We must face up to this discrepancy honestly. Message and challenge are intended at the same time for the messenger too, he is both messenger and hearer.

There is a temptation either to act in naïve self-deception, as though we really were what the message declares and demands, or to pull God's message down to our own level and to fashion it according to our own standard *(diminutae sunt veritates a filiis hominum)*. St. Paul lived in consciousness of this discrepancy between his weakness and the dignity and majesty of his mission.

Both are there in his writings: weak vessel and precious content, poor creature and the apostle of Jesus Christ, the messenger of the great King.

2. Invitation

"But all things are of God, who hath reconciled us to himself by Christ and hath given to us the ministry of reconciliation. For God indeed was in Christ, reconciling the world to himself, not imputing to them their sins. And he hath placed in us the word of reconciliation. For Christ therefore we are ambassadors, God as it were exhorting through us. For Christ, we beseech you, be reconciled to God" (1 Cor. 5:18–21).

The content of the sermon is "the word of reconciliation", the invitation: "Be reconciled to God!" It is a repeated reminder of the hand of God outstretched for our reconciliation. Even more literally and profoundly, it is God's wooing of us. "The kingdom of heaven is likened to a king who made a marriage for his son." Christ is the bridegroom. In the images of the Last Day at the end of the Apocalypse it is written: "The marriage of the Lamb has come. Blessed are they that are called to the marriage supper of the Lamb!" The sermon is the wooing for the consent of the bride which must be spoken anew again and again. John is the "friend of the bridegroom". The sermon is the wooing of the friend of the bridegroom for the bride: "That (Christ) might present it to himself, a glorious Church, not having spot or wrinkle or any such thing, but that it should be holy and without blemish." The sermon is both the invitation to the wedding of the Lamb and the wooing for the love of the bride.

It is from this that the discrepancy comes between a solicitous and compliant patience and a dignity which does not run after anyone nor throw itself away; between "shake off the dust from your feet" and "to be all things to all men in order to win a few for Christ".

The preacher is therefore not just an indifferent messenger, but the bearer of an invitation in which he joins with all his heart.

3. Witness

The preacher as messenger tells of invisible reality, of future events. As suitor he tells of an invisible, mysterious and hidden love which often seems in contradiction with life. The message, therefore, must be upheld by the credibility of the messenger; the message must be corroborated by the witness of the messenger. He has to be both messenger and witness, his word must be credible and convincing. Today this is of particular importance, especially in those parts where Catholics are few. The faithful too are constantly in a state of spiritual choice. They hunger for confirmation of their faith from a credible witness.

The sermon is at the same time an attestation. In some way or other we must make the whole of life its background. Somehow the people must be able to sense that the preacher himself really has staked all on this card; that he really does order his life in full acceptance of God's authority and recognizes it as a reality; that he has really taken upon himself the venture of faith. It is not "perfection" which is asked, but aspiration towards the union between faith and life: the readiness to vouch for his message and to take all its consequences upon himself. We must be able to feel that here it is not fine words which count, but an inner decision.

150

4. Nourishment

Faith is life – therefore it needs nourishment. The sermon, especially the regular Sunday sermon, is first and foremost the nourishment for faith: *In tempore tritici mensuram* – at the right time the right measure of corn. "Not in bread alone doth man live but in every word that proceedeth from the mouth of God." The priest is the spiritual father of the house, the steward whom the Lord has set over his family that he may give it "at the right time the right measure of corn". These people it is then, who must be able to live by it; it must be wholesome, enjoyable and digestible food for them. There is no objective criterion. The same sermon can be good in one place and bad in another. The distinction must be made between 'milk' and 'solid food'; between the real food content and the stimulating extras; between cake and bread. The judgment of the listeners may confuse the issue. The question we must ask ourselves is: Do I really give them a sound and nourishing diet from which the faith of men can really live and grow in the world in which they find themselves, in their kind of atmosphere, among the burdens which weigh upon them? The heavier the burden of faith and the more destructive the atmosphere, the more important is strong and sound nourishment, if faith is not to become weak and ailing. Another relevant question is: What are the minimum "iron rations" which I must give? "Dry bread" is far from being the answer. Appetizing food has its uses too, providing we do not forget what matters ultimately.

Is there not probably more hunger than we realize? People do listen when they notice that you really have something to say and really mean it. Ought not the faithful to look forward to

Sunday once more with 'appetite', indeed with an inner hunger? Today they do so far more than formerly; it is then the more important that we do not disappoint them.

Every sermon should contain these four elements, albeit in varying combinations and with different emphases.

Do we take preaching seriously enough? Do we leave ourselves enough time for it? What secret expectations may be at work among our audience, what past and future experiences! Most people today are in some way or other having to make decisions of a fundamental sort. In the first instance we should feel dismayed at the task of speaking convincingly to people such as these about God and his kingdom. There is something wrong somewhere if we find it too easy!

But it is also rewarding to know that we have something to say when others are silent, that we have nothing to alter or to retract. We speak to men of the things that ultimately matter.

16

Holy Scripture in the Life of the Parish

ALFONS KIRCHGAESSNER

IT is unnecessary to prove to the reader of this book the importance of Holy Scripture for the liturgy, for the community
and for the individual. Therefore we will confine ourselves to
indicating a few practical suggestions that may lead towards a
greater knowledge and acceptance of Holy Scripture.

The first, of course, is and remains the divine service; above
all the Mass, which has as its basis the texts of Holy Scripture.
The general hope for a new arrangement of the pericopes (a
three- or four-year plan) is based not only on the desire that
Catholic Christians should in this way become familiar with the
most important passages of the Old and New Testaments, but
also on the experience that the annually recurring pericopes
are no longer listened to with real attention by many people,
because "they know them already". Another certainly well
founded motive is that preachers might be encouraged to use
the Scriptures more extensively.

In any case, we might in this way recapture that ideal situation, when the sermon really is a homily, an explanation of the
text of the Scriptures and of its practical application to life. Many
preachers dodge the issue by talking about a dogmatic or a
moral topic, because they don't want to or feel that they can't
talk every year about the Raising of the Widow's Son or the

Feeding of the Five Thousand. The sermon on the Scriptures, in which the basic truths of Revelation and the key-words of the liturgy are brought home to the people, is unfortunately no longer general and accepted practice—quite in contrast to Protestant worship. The embellishment of sermons with quotations from the Scriptures or examples from sacred history is a poor substitute. If the Book of Books is to become once again the book of life for the faithful, it must be opened for them Sunday after Sunday. Then the gulf between liturgy and sermon, between the Scripture and everyday life will disappear. It is useless to repeat the admonition frequently addressed to preachers that they must penetrate more deeply into the world of the Bible by private study of the relevant commentaries. The embarrassing question what to preach about would disappear as soon as one could draw upon the riches of the New and Old Testament. The chief need for initiating the parish into the life of Scripture and teaching them how to live from it, is the daily study of the Bible. This must, of course, go considerably beyond the devout recitation of the psalms of the Breviary and the reading of the Latin texts in the Missal and the Office. Many complaints about sermons today and about the spirituality of priests would be silenced if the Bible once again became their favourite book.

The meditation that is obligatory upon priests ought to follow the Scripture readings; and might well take the little book of Spiritual Exercises as a classic model. A meditation on the pericope for the following Sunday would prove an important part of the sermon preparation; for it is obvious that such a text has to be prayed as well as understood for the proper preaching of the faith.

154

Readings from Holy Scripture are now provided for afternoon devotions in many new German hymn-books. This is regarded as an important complement to the morning's events, though only relatively few of the faithful may be reached in this way. But among these few are often those who hunger for spiritual nourishment and who have a right to be led further into the world of the Bible. Vespers, like Compline, also offer an opportunity to read out an unfamiliar text from the Bible and to talk about it.

It is heartening to note a great deal of space being devoted in these new German hymn-books to the psalms and psalmodic hymns. Every parish priest should encourage their use in practice too. Without doubt the devotional life of our people will receive new stimulus and impetus when the singing and praying of the psalms becomes once again a matter of course. A beginning should be made with first communicants; here, for example, the psalm "The Lord is my shepherd" presents itself as an outstandingly suitable text. Experience shows that small children like saying or singing a prayer like this not only in class but at home too. Priests should also have recourse to the psalms more often than they do when giving penances, for the psalms really have some message for every spiritual condition and every understanding.

Biblical topics could and should be among those treated at some of the various parish meetings (I do not here mean the purely social ones). They must, of course, be put across in a popular and interesting form. We know from experience that lantern-slides are popular; and there is a real abundance of slides on biblical subjects. Attractive subjects are, for example, the journeys made by St. Paul; Palestine, Land and People; old and new Bible illustrations; characters from the Bible by famous painters. The discoveries at Qumran, too, and every-thing connected with them as well as questions of apologetics (Infallibility of the Bible; the Bible and science; the Bible and historical research) will meet with interest.

The teaching of the faith, in whatever form it is presented to young people or adults, should also take its inspiration from the Bible; indeed it could use a Gospel or Epistel as the basic text for certain parts of the course.

As far as actual "Bible study" groups are concerned, which on the Catholic side are only as old as the Liturgical Movement (it seems now somewhat premature to have spoken of a "Biblical Movement"), I have had experience of them throughout the twenty-six years of my priesthood. In hard times they meant a lot to us, and many people still remember our war-time group readings of the Epistle to the Romans and the Gospel of St. John. My post-war experience in my own parish and elsewhere in Germany do not dispose me to be optimistic; the circle of interested people remains very small – thirty to forty in a parish of 7500 people; but old women and those "pious souls", who come joyfully to anything to do with the church, are in the majority. In spite of this it is a unique opportunity and perhaps one should persevere even when the number of those attending is disappointing, simply for the sake of the few eager and inquiring minds – and not least for the sake of the rich personal rewards. The most valuable thing in the Bible study groups is the atmosphere of reverent attention to God's Word. This atmosphere of prayer is often helped by a final summary in form of a prayer. For the sake of this atmosphere one might dispense with points for discussion during the study hour and at least postpone them till the end.

156

Finally I should like to indicate the possibility of putting some striking Scriptural text (hand-written perhaps in an artistic way) on the church notice-board as Protestants have done for a long time; perhaps a passer-by or one of "our people" will be impressed by it; though this is not anything that can either be foreseen or recorded afterwards. In any case we should open every conceivable approach by which the Bible can reach men. When we want to give a present to our servers or on the occasion of a silver wedding or to deserving people at Christmas, why should it not be a copy of the New Testament or the Psalms? We should not rest until the Book of Books is to be found in every family – and is read there.

17

The Mystagogical Sermon

ROMANO GUARDINI

I

ACCORDING to the early Christian view, Christian existence depends on the continuous intervention of God. This intervention forms sacred history which is enacted all through secular history. Its content is the hidden development of the new man, of the "new heaven and new earth", until the time when the Lord will come again and reveal all things. The liturgy is the most striking representation of these events. But as far as the sermon is concerned, it is not restricted to the liturgical sphere though deeply rooted in it.

In modern times this conception has changed. Our era, even when it believes, no longer sees the world as something proceeding directly from the hand of God but as an entity which may have been created by him, but which is now functioning according to its own laws. Correspondingly, the focal point of the spiritual life is shifting away from God's mysterious universal intervention, the objective of which is the final Revelation, towards the inner life of the individual, his thoughts, feelings and attitudes. The liturgy is no longer conceived as the most important point of intersection and continuous manifestation of that sacred history, but as a means of edification. The sermon loses to a large extent its aspect as a religious cult and enters the general human and intellectual sphere. To a large extent it is no longer expression and instrument of the *opus Dei* and becomes the voice of the priest as teacher who presents ideas, appeals to feelings, and invokes decisions of the will. It touches science on the one hand and literature on the other.

For some time now another change has seemed to be taking place. The certainty and self-confidence of the modern outlook have been undermined. Man feels the indecisiveness of existence, the unforeseeable nature of events and the incalculability of his own potentialities. Reality is experienced elementally and lessens the importance of mere knowledge and experience. The decisive factor in the question of God's existence lies not in the ideal or the intuitive but in how God attests his presence and the place he takes in the lives of the faithful. The future of Christian existence would seem to depend upon how far the Christian learns to see God at work in this so intensely real world; to feel that God is still more powerful and more real than this world; and to give the world back into God's hand, as it were, and to understand himself in the light of God's creativity and activity. Whereas at the beginning of the modern era "knowledge" was synonymous with "thinking", now seeing, hearing, touching and acting seem to be acquiring a completely new significance. "Knowledge" has come once more out of the derivative sphere (that is, the sphere of concepts) into the sphere of primary experience, of the senses, which thereby acquire a totally new authority. The old saying "There is nothing in the intellect which was not first in the senses" contains a meaning far and away above that credited to it either by Idealism on the one hand or Positivism on the other. The senses cease to be the

159

humble instruments of the intellect – which idea again presupposed that the "mind" alone was regarded as the basis of knowledge and the "body" merely its indispensable substratum. The whole man has become the focal point. It is not the "mind" but the "man" who knows. What he knows is not concepts but reality; but the organs with which he comes into contact with reality are the senses. The senses are man in so far as it is his aim to complete this contact with reality: a unity of mind and body; and if one accepts, in addition, the old theory of the "inner" and "spiritual" senses, the acts and objects of the senses range throughout the whole breadth, height and depth of reality.

From this point of view the liturgy takes on an entirely new urgency. Its task is not to elucidate the ideas of dogma, to edify the mind or to impart spiritual and aesthetic feelings. It is the living act in which the workings of God are manifested to the eyes, ears and hands of men; the sphere of existence into which men are taken up and re-created for a new life.

Liturgy is above all action: its crucial act is the enactment of the Mass. The individual is drawn into this enactment; he takes his meaning from it; he is comprehended and formed by it. Thus the sermon, too, gains a new meaning. It is not merely religious teaching which could in itself be expounded anywhere and which is bound up with public worship simply because the community comes together for this regularly and is then in a particularly receptive state of mind; on the contrary, it is connected in the most intimate way with the liturgical events themselves. The sermon originates in the liturgy and leads back to the liturgy, serves to unfold it and indeed constitutes one part of the enactment. Naturally there are also other varied forms of

160

independent instruction from the evening sermon to the talk in the parish hall; just as important as these, however, if not the essential and most important, is that preaching of the holy Truth which is embedded in the liturgy and forms a part of it.

II

The connection of the sermon with the liturgical action may be achieved in various ways. One of these is when the Epistle or Gospel of the Mass is interpreted – provided, of course, that they really are interpreted and not taken as a starting-point for developing some idea or other as though it were a musical theme. The homily, which endeavours to explain the text according to its context and content, is indeed by far the most important form of the sermon. In taking the day's texts as its subject and basing its entire attitude on the mood of the Mass, the sermon gains a true liturgical character. It is then presenting the words and message which it was the duty of the head of the Eucharistic celebration to present, when he told the participants in the sacred meal of the life and work of him who would afterwards come among them, when they enacted the commemoration of the Lord. In any case this presupposes the realization of an old and very urgent desire: the wider extension of the system of pericopes. The present cycle of readings is restricted to a single year. Since, moreover, several Sundays have been displaced by feasts, the number of biblical texts is small and sermons easily tend to be repetitive. This situation must clearly be remedied. The present cycle of readings could itself remain unaltered – although some readings have shifted from their proper places and would have to be restored to them – but two or three further cycles could be added so as to provide a choice. Then the riches of Holy Scripture in our Sunday and Holy Day Masses would be used to best advantage and the preacher would have a greater possibility of using the resources of the liturgy in his sermon.

I must mention here another particularly effective type of liturgical sermon. I mean one which is directly at the service of the liturgical action, the "mystagogical" sermon. It can act as preparation for the sacred actions or occur within them at a definite moment or make them awaken echoes in the soul. From many years' experience I should like to put forward a few examples.

III

My first attempt arose out of the reflection that when the prayers at the foot of the altar begin, the faithful are as yet very little prepared for the sacred actions. They are more or less in the same state as they were outside the church door or on their way from home. They are distracted and often, in fact, have no truly devout attitude at all. Above all, the feeling of a "community" is lacking. This community does not consist merely of a certain number of devoutly inclined individuals but of a living whole which is the foundation for the sacred act. In this act the Church – the greater "whole" of all the faithful extending throughout the whole world – becomes present. This community cannot, however, come about of itself; therefore it is the responsibility of religious instruction to see that it does – above all, by the priest's giving a short instruction at the beginning of Mass, which is designed entirely for this purpose. This can have very different starting-points: the problem of concentration or the liturgical symbols – or the Mass itself, its meaning as a whole as much as its individual parts.

Such an address contributes directly towards creating among the more or less devout individuals an inner unity which supports the subsequent sacred action. Continued over a longer period, it has a profound and far-reaching effect. The actual sermon within the Mass itself will then also have a far greater effect.

A truly mystagogical sermon does not try to set out sacred doctrine or improve morals or give religious edification in the general sense, but to create that disposition without which the faithful cannot really collaborate in the liturgical act; to appeal to something which can originate only from the living believing act, namely, the community. It is quite clear, too, that it in no way supersedes the sermon within the Mass itself.

IV

The baptismal address will serve as a second example. Here a first essential is that the administration of the sacrament should be accorded its rightful significance, which is often overlooked. Naturally this is partly due to external causes: the frequency with which the sacrament is administered, the priest's burden of work and similar factors. The real reason, however, is probably that in the general consciousness baptism has lost the importance which is its due. As soon as it is once again seen more clearly for what it is, the liturgical enactment of the "rebirth of water and the Holy Ghost", matters will change of

11*   163 their own accord. There are no real impossibilities here. The true meaning of baptism depends not on theoretical speculation about it or occasional references to it, but on genuine feeling and desire.

Our modern baptismal service presents the extremely abbreviated outline of a rite which once had a wealth of detail and extended over a longer period. Therefore we must ask ourselves whether what is essential in the ceremony is clear and obvious, whether the individual symbols can be understood and what could be done to make this so. A further question would be whether the dignity of the rite is increased if several baptisms are performed together and the whole ceremony given a more solemn form. Perhaps from time to time baptisms could be held on Sunday afternoon instead of devotions and performed when the whole parish could be there; they could be combined with an address and the faithful could take part with appropriate prayers and hymns.

Let us presume then, that the child is carried by someone who is both willing and sympathetic and that the god-parents, family and friends are all gathered together; and yet even then there is still no real baptismal community. Above all, the men present generally feel embarrassed. They must be helped to face the situation with equanimity. Apart from this, the feelings which move those present are of a very vague sort.

Usually they will simply be family feelings: joy at the newly-born child, pride in the son and heir, satisfaction or anxiety because of the growing number of children, and so on. The more reflective among those present will be moved by the fact that a human life has begun and will be aware of a destiny as yet unknown. The baptismal address has to convert all this into the liturgical sphere; to lead men from the familiar and human to what is holy.

The address should start from the human situation and give it its due; the things which touch most nearly the hearts of those present should be put into words. Then we should say: All this is not the really essential thing; for this lies deeper. It does not consist merely in the consecration of what is human and familiar. Its essentials can only be understood in the light of God's word.

We could also start from the inner structure of the baptismal ceremony: its individual rites and symbols; the Christian responsibility of the god-parents; the growth of the inner life of the soul in the midst of daily life; life's fulfilment in the Resurrection and the Judgment and so on. The only important thing is that the address should not put the emphasis on doctrine or ethics, but should try to lead those present away from their familiar everyday attitude towards a liturgical one and so make the sacred actions accessible to them.

v

The mystagogical sermon cannot be introduced arbitrarily. Since it is intimately bound up with the liturgical action, it must be justified by it. Perhaps the following occasions where it is suitable should be mentioned.

Above all, there are the two occasions which play such an important part in the life of the community, that is, marriage and burial. People's conception of these events, too, has in many cases degenerated into something purely human and everyday. It is a question of giving the address a liturgical form, as the

165

introduction to a holy act in which divine mystery and human life intermingle. The preacher must understand the nature of human life with its hopes and fears and show how it is drawn into the domain of divine mystery. He will then relate it all in a fruitful way to the liturgical action.

At a wedding he can treat in this way of the entry of the couple into the church from outside, from the confusions of human life; the procession up to the altar and its mystery, which from now on guards, as it were, the roots of the new bond for life; the solemn questions of the priest who represents the Church and the answer of the bridal couple with all the decision and responsibility that goes with it; the symbolism of the ring, the blessing as an expression of divine power and favour, as a protection throughout life, a guarantee of fruitfulness, and so on.

At a burial he should speak of the tranquillity of death, which the coffin itself seems to express; the symbolism of the earth from which God formed the human body; the connection between grave and baptism and also between grave and resurrection; the life now at its end and the new life which is coming; the community gathering round the grave and the common link between them of man's last end; the impenetrability of the future and the fact that we are all in God's hand . . .

Confession, too, can provide an occasion for the mystagogical sermon; at least it can when there is some sort of community, as, for instance, at a Children's Confession. Every priest knows how barren and monotonous a child's confession often is. This may be connected with the problem of the formation and examination of conscience, neither of which can be discussed here; but it is also connected with the fact that in the mind of the

166

community confession has taken on an almost exclusively moral character. The child feels that the most important and worrying thing is whether he "says everything correctly". It is this which almost completely ousts the truly sacral element, which sees confession as forming a sacred environment which envelops the penitent with its depth and greatness; which sees something creative and mysterious and past human understanding taking place in confession: forgiveness and a new beginning. Confession would take on an entirely new character if the priest said something about this mystery at the beginning. There are various aspects from which he might start. Above all, he should begin with the fundamentals of confession, in which everything that is hidden, oppressive and secret comes out into the open, not simply in front of someone or other but in front of the representative of God, so that the confession is taken up into the openness that is God's. Or else a sermon might deal with the priest's hearing and understanding of confession; with the answer he gives to it and with the all-comprehending love of God which is at work in everything. Or again how confession makes a break with what is past, how from then on life begins anew and how in confession the mystery in baptism is made effective. How hope is given by this new beginning, how in human terms it becomes tired by failures, yet is ever strengthened anew and made sure, because God is involved too. It could deal with moral aspiration and progress and its difficulties and setbacks, but seen in the context of God's infinite wisdom, infinite goodness and creative grace which are expressed in the Sacrament of Penance, and so on. Through instruction such as this, the human and moral content of confession is bound up with the sacramental act; they each shed light on the other

167

and the act which follows becomes a living one. It would be worthy of closer examination how far many of the defects in the life of the conscience, especially overscrupulousness and narrowness, are connected with the one-sided moralizing of confession and could therefore be removed by the development of its liturgical and sacramental character.

Other occasions, too, will occur, when a mystagogical talk can be given. But here no rules can be established. The priest must keep his eyes open and have his parish's welfare at heart; then he will notice what is needed.

In the earlier days of Christianity the form of the liturgical actions was clear and complete. The faithful had the ability of classical times to watch, to listen and to co-enact. The catechumen comprehended the different rites, with which baptism and admission into the Church were completed, not only with his thoughts but also and especially with his eyes, his ears and his gestures, with his entire, living being. So to teach was simply to point and say: "That is what you have seen, that is what has happened to you, that is what you have done." There was no need to convey or correlate ideas in a complicated way, for it was enough to point and say: "That is that." Gradually, however, the forms of the sacred action lost their first clarity and power. They shrivelled up and sometimes very little remained. Things that did not belong to it accumulated; its inner structure was altered. Thus the meaning of a ceremony can, in most cases, no longer be understood simply by seeing and acting. Apart from that, modern man no longer has the ability of classical times to hear, to see and to grasp with the hands and to learn through action. Reason has obtruded and with it its opposite, subjective emotion. The will has disassociated itself and claimed independence; the heart has become dull and the instinct uncertain. Even in the Middle Ages the allegorical approach to the liturgy had begun – for instance, in the writings of Sicardus and Durandus, who no longer really explain (that is, make the phenomenon speak) but associate theoretical ideas with liturgical things by all sorts of analogical references. The modern age finally no longer sees, hears and enacts the liturgy, but thinks and feels it, adopts it as a means of edification and as a basis for ethical decisions.

It is here that work must be begun. The forms of the liturgical actions must be brought out as clearly and completely as possible. At the same time a form of interpretative and educative communication must be found which does not explain or admonish but sets free the inner senses, leads men into the sacred act, and brings about its consummation.

169

18

Active Participation in the Mass

BALTHASAR FISCHER

RECENTLY I picked up an old German explanation of the Mass, printed in red and black and written in old-fashioned language. In it the "pious reader" is constantly admonished: "When you are behind a Mass; do this, pray that." Suddenly it was clear to me what it was that used to be so distressing about our churches: the people behaved as though they were standing or kneeling "behind" a Mass, like pious (and perhaps even silent) spectators of a sacred play. Not that they would have thought little of the Mass; it was something holy and precious to them. This was what they had learnt from their mother, this was how they thought of it and this was certainly praiseworthy enough in comparison with the many, all too many today, who no longer even know what the inside of a church looks like. But when on Sunday morning they said: "We are going to Mass", they really only meant the auditorium of the Mass – the Mass, the sacrifice itself, was celebrated and offered up by the priest, they thought. Although they would no longer have put it like this, they had the feeling of being "behind" the Mass.

In recent decades, thank God, things have been very different in most of the churches in Germany, even if, unfortunately, not in all. Today when you go into a church on Sunday, you are aware even after a few minutes from the joyful sound of the people's responses, from their singing and praying, from their standing and kneeling that here the faithful know that they are not "behind" the Mass but in its midst. They are once again fully conscious that because the priest plays the chief rôle, the title rôle of Christ, in this sacred drama, they themselves are not therefore spectators but real and proper co-actors.

Anyone who has ever been present at a Mass in Rome in one of the big old basilicas, perhaps even at a Papal Mass, could not possibly conceive the idea that he was "behind" the Mass. For throughout the Mass the celebrant is facing him.

It is a real joy that not infrequently our bishops too now give priests permission to have Mass in this way, facing the people. Then suddenly the false idea of our being "behind" the Mass is destroyed, as it were, at one blow. Then we can sense immediately: that's not his Mass, that the priest is saying out there in front of us, it's ours. Like the father of a family, he is going to distribute to us God's sacred Word and God's sacred Bread from this holy table.

But even when the priest is looking with us towards the altar, let us not, whatever we do, take this as a desire on his part to turn away from us, to do something that does not concern us. Admittedly we are, in this case, behind the priest, but we are a long way from being behind the Mass. When you walk in a procession you are certainly behind the cross-bearer, but for that very reason you are in the middle of the procession. The Mass is like one great procession which goes towards Christ, and with him towards the Heavenly Father, with the priest at its head. Or to express it by another image: we are behind the priest in the same way that mountain-climbers are behind their leader. We are not watching from below as he climbs the

171

mountain and greets us, as it were, from above. We are climbing with him to the summit of Christ's oblation, and when he constantly turns round, he does so because, like a good leader, he wants to make sure that we are following him, because he wants to spur us on lest we tire on the difficult ascent.

It is a holy joy and a real blessing that the faithful everywhere are now themselves taking over once again their sacred right which for all too long they left to the boy servers out in front at the altar. It is dangerous to allow a fundamental right to be exercised for centuries only by a delegate – in the end you no longer know that it is really you who are entitled to it. We should be grateful to the great popes, St. Pius X, Pius XI and Pius XII, that they never tired of pointing out to the faithful their holy and fundamental right, acquired in baptism, of being co-offerers in the Mass. Again and again they urged that the people should play this their part once again, should think, act, pray, sing, offer and, most important of all, eat jointly with the priest at the holy table.

I said it was comforting that here in Germany the faithful are listening with increasing eagerness to the voices of the chief shepherds of the Church and that they are at last taking over once again their part in the Mass. In spite of this I must admit that I have one worry. However wonderfully everything "goes off without a hitch" at our Masses, however well the faithful know the words of their rôle "by heart", this is far from being enough. Fundamentally the problem is an entirely different one, the problem of an "inner" knowledge. The words of the mouth must come from the depths of the heart, must be an inner prayer, otherwise even the most "liturgical" Mass is nothing but sounding brass or a tinkling cymbal and an abomination before the face of the Lord. I believe that we all have something to learn here, that we have to learn our "parts" with one another. All the magnificent texts which the priest speaks in the Mass, however rewarding they might be, we will put on one side. We will only aim at learning to understand more deeply the very few, very simple words which are given to us, which belong to the people's part in the sacred ceremony. We will reflect upon them together, so that they become not only the voice of our mouth but increasingly the voice of our heart too, so that they penetrate more and more into our flesh and blood, until one day in the most profound sense we will truly know them "by heart".

19

The Table of the Lord

Heinrich Kahlefeld

The Sacraments of the Church have the appearance of sacred enactments. We see them as a bath of purification, as a laying on of hands and anointing, as a judicial process, as a meal which is sanctified through thanksgiving.

The Sacrament of the Eucharist does not only consist in the sacred enactment; the object of the action too, the centre of the act, is made available sacramentally in it: the Flesh and Blood of the Lord given for us in his death on the Cross.

This is the source of a new responsibility for the Church: sacred truths, in the form of sacred things, are entrusted to her; she must know how to use them and how to preserve them. What is entrusted to her is the Flesh and Blood of the Lord; but it is given to her under the appearances of bread and wine. So in order to contain, carry and elevate it, she needs vessels for the bread and wine. These are the plates for the bread (paten, dish, ciborium) and the cup for the wine (chalice).

Like our ordinary bread-plates and wine-glasses they are carried around and lifted up. They stand on a table and the table is laid for the meal; for bread is given us to eat and wine to drink.

When the "Lord's supper" (1 Cor. 11) begins after the service of the Word, bread and wine are brought and placed upon the table; next the thanksgiving is said over the bread and wine and then those taking part in the celebration eat the food from the communal table. This is the "Lord's supper". Under these actions the Lord preserves for his Church the presence of the sacrifice of his death made to God his Father, so that she may enter into it and take life from it. And so the table bearing the bread and wine is the "Lord's table" (1 Cor. 10) and the "altar" of the sacrifice of Christ.

Thus the altar in our churches is first of all an object, an instrument, a simple thing that has its usefulness and its rightness and a meaning clear to anyone who knows what is signified by a table, a table covered with a cloth, with food on it. Even though it is not part of the sacrament, its significance is just as effective as that of the bread and the wine. If it is no more than a good, strong, worthy table, it is appropriate and acceptable to God; for the simple bread from the wheat and the wine from the grape were acceptable to God.

The altar too is a sign, a basis and pre-requisite for the sacramental sign of the bread and wine; it should remain visible as this sign in spite of all ornamentation and design. If it is nothing but a table, it has in its very simplicity a particular power to speak – in sign language; it points far beyond itself to the divine mystery which it supports and serves.

Following upon this basis, which must never be discarded, there is a second aspect, which presents the reverse. The cup which holds the species of the wine was at first made of glass or wood, but today it is of silver or gold, the skill of goldsmiths and decorations of precious stones indicating its excellence. The paten, too, is of gold and in the Greek Church an arc like that of the heaven's bends above it and the Star of Bethlehem hangs

175

from it, telling of the King that has come. In the Western Church the breads for the altar are unleavened wafers, baked between heated irons, bright and shining; some pious emblems, such as the crucifix and the letters IHS, are stamped on it. The Greeks treat the bread at the Offertory of their Lord's Supper as if it were, in appearance too, the Body of the Lord: they pierce it through the centre with a small lance.

What is the meaning of all this?

Here the first and primary "significance", inherent in the object chosen by God and raised to a sacrament, is overshadowed by a second and lesser significance arising from the soul and the imaginative faculty of man. The soul of the believer perceives the inner reality of the sacrament, the *"res"*, and aspires to a sense representation of what it has perceived. So the second, artificial significance develops; it moves, as it were downwards, on the same plane as the primary significance is moving upwards; that is, it does not limit itself, say, to raising the cross meaningfully above the table, and then behind it, on the church wall or in a painting, expressing what happens on the altar; it refashions the form of the bread, the dish for the bread and also the cup and then the table which holds them.

We may say then, that the secondary significance is given the more room for development, the further the object which it wishes to remould is from the strictly circumscribed appearance of the sacrament. The bread must be bread, the wine must be wine, otherwise the sacrament is invalid. But the appearance of the table can be completely remoulded.

What does this secondary significance aim to express of the sacramental reality? Precisely the essence of any cult, the thing in which it finds its highest concentration and final truth:

176

sacrifice. The altar belongs to the sacrifice as the "place of slaughter" or the "place of fire".

As soon as they had grasped the difference between the New and the Old Covenant and its consequences, the early Christian generations only spoke of the "altar" with awe and aloofness or in clearly non-actual terms, just as they avoided the name "priest". They could not afford to let the power of the Lord be overshadowed; their religious teaching had to stress that there is only one sacrifice, which the Lord offered on the cross once and for all, a sacrifice of inexhaustible fruitfulness. One sacrifice: this death of salvation. One priest: Christ the Lord. So, too, one altar: that is, figuratively, the cross of Christ; or precisely and literally: his Body, he himself; for he was everything: priest, oblation and place of sacrifice. "The sanctuary into which Jesus has entered is not one made by human hands, is not some adumbration of the truth; he has entered heaven itself . . . It is his own blood, not the blood of goats and calves, that has enabled him to enter, once for all, the sanctuary . . . Nor does he make a repeated offering of himself, as the high priest . . . makes a yearly offering of the blood that is not his own . . . In accordance with this divine will we have been sanctified by an offering made once for all, the body of Jesus Christ" (Heb. 9:24, 12, 25; 10:10).

The Church's inheritance, by which her worship of God achieves motive and focal point, is of a sacramental nature. Her priesthood is sacramental: it is an instrument the service of which is in participating in the priesthood of Christ; her sacrifice is sacramental: participation in the sacrifice of Christ made actual under a sign. The sacramental signs are bread and wine and what happens over them and with them: the thanksgiving and the meal. The form of the table is in keeping with this.

When, however, the Old Testament and pagan sacrifices were no longer near enough to exercise any influence or be a source of confusion, and the fact that there is only one Priest of the New Covenant was firmly and clearly established, the elders and leaders, who are made instruments of the Lord by the laying on of hands, could also, by reason of their participation, be called "priests". On the same lines it was possible, too, to describe the table, the mensa, as "altar" in order to give the sacrificial service a witness and sign.

How did this come about? Probably the flat mensa stone was laid on a block which was itself raised up above the ground on steps – resembling the mountain-top from which the sacrifice was offered up to the divinity. Through this secondary symbolic function which is non-sacramental but interpretative and procla- matory, the table received a new dignity and splendour.

In the primary significance the movement was upwards: as a proper table it bore the food and told of the mystery of faith as being a meal; it stood there without itself belonging to the sacramental form, yet it was in the extending line of sacramental symbolization; it helped, on its own level and in its own place, to establish the sign bearing the reality of God. It also told of the meal and the food and also of the consecra- tion of the food; for it was empty and asked for bread and wine to be laid upon it, so that leaving the human sphere the bread and wine might enter into the sphere of Christ's eucharistic prayer and hence into the divine sphere – and from there would be received back again.

Next, however, the movement is downwards. The divine reality, which the sign bears and which the eye of faith recog- nizes, communicates its splendour to the lowly table. In the light of this divine reality, faith has a new and different vision of the table, just as the prophet Isaias in his vision saw the upper beams of the temple in a new light: they no longer supported the roof of the house but the throne of God and trembled beneath the might which weighed upon them.

The vision of faith has refashioned the form of the table, made it into an "altar", has regarded it even as the Lord himself, has seen its cloths as the linen for the Lord's body, the ornamentation on the material which covers the stone as his royal robes. Here faith has employed its knowledge to interpret what was already there, has expressed this interpretation symbolically and perfected it according to the principles of symbolism. So the dignity of the table, of which the faithful are conscious because they are able to understand the primary symbols, is represented to their enlightened senses by secondary symbols.

What practical conclusions can we draw from these facts?

First, that the altar can be constructed as a simple *mensa*, a table. It is the responsibility of the architect to see that the outer form of the table is proportioned to the area around it and to the congregation that will surround it, and thereby to give expression to its dignity.

We have already mentioned that the form of the table, though simple and solid itself, must be of a certain richness both in material and in design. Simplicity must not be confused with poverty. Nor should it be thought that the "table" is a matter for the "joiner" and him alone. He must be a true artist. Music offers a parallel: the greatest and most difficult of the skills of composition is the art of creating a tune.

It is also evident that the altar can be represented as *bomos*, the place of sacrifice. This will probably be the case with regard to the high altar in most parish-churches. Probably, however, there will be a chapel or apse or some other smaller area in such a church, where Mass is said on weekdays with a smaller attendance, so that these, too, can be a "congregation"; this is the place for the "table". Then the one form of altar would interpret the other and instruction on the Lord's Supper, its symbol and reality, would be easy to give: the people could look and see for themselves.

In addition, one or two conclusions may be drawn about the care and decoration of the altar. Decoration should not be independent of its object; it must specifically decorate the altar. The altar should not be overloaded with flowers until it looks like a florist's shop. The flowers on it must take second place to the sacred vessels for the bread and wine and the priest's handling of them. They should beautify without distracting the attention, like flowers on a festive table. The candles, too, should not detract from the form of the altar; their function is an even more truly auxiliary one. It is not economy, but a sense of rightness which makes the Church direct that six candles should burn at High Mass. Anyone who has tried it will know that twelve candles are less, not more, effective than six. Should more be needed for Benediction, they can easily be added later. For on the evening before the altar is not being prepared for Benediction (at which it has no necessary function as a table) but for the celebration of Mass and, above all, for High Mass.

But a greater feast may certainly merit a greater number of candles. St. Luke relates of the celebration of the breaking of bread in Troas (Acts 20:8): "And there were a great number of lamps in the upper chamber where we were assembled." But on such occasions the candles should not stand on the table used for the Mass: they should decorate the walls, or be carried in the hand, or large numbers might be grouped together to give a festive appearance, towering up on tall staffs in a large circle round the altar, as is done in the Chapel of Christ the King in the cathedral of Fulda in Germany.

In some cathedral churches, where, as is well known, the Sacrament is usually kept not on the High Altar but on a special altar in a side chapel, lamps burn continuously round the High Altar. They are of plain glass and thus distinguishable from the Sanctuary Lamp; they burn round the altar as they might before a holy picture.

This brings us to the care of the altar. Care does not merely mean the things that are done as a matter of course: that the linen should be meticulously clean and the candlesticks polished, etc., but that the dignity and appearance of the altar should be enhanced.

This can be done first of all by its form and by its position in the church. The dignity of the altar should, after all, radiate to all parts of the church; in order to enhance its position as the focus of attention, it will be necessary to take a look from the altar at the lines of radiation into the church; various things will have to be changed, until the altar really is the focal point of attention from every part of the church.

It can also be done by the way in which the celebrating priest and his servers behave towards the altar, above all during Mass but also at other times too. The faithful are not blind; they can see what is done at the altar and know instinctively its significance – and for their part they learn, as it were spontaneously, to pay the altar the reverence which is its due, as the permanent symbol of the most sacred actions.

181

20

The Altar

FERDINAND KOLBE

INSIDE a church nothing approaches the importance of the altar. For churches were built so that communities could gather together in the name of Christ and in commemoration of him; this happens chiefly at the altar.

Its purpose, as the place for the Eucharistic mystery, makes it of itself a sacred place, indeed it symbolizes Christ himself.

We must, however, realize that there is very little feeling for the great value of the altar as manifested in the liturgy and as nourished by it in the mind of the people. This must be awakened once again – by instruction as much as by the appearance presented by the altars constructed today, by their furnishings and the way they are cared for, and not least by the reverence shown to the altar by the servers.

More important than all questions of design and furnishings is the position of the altar in the church. It must make clear and visible that the altar is "the heart of the Church , the focal point at which all lines converge".[1] So it is understandable that often today the choir is given a new design and the altar a new position, even in churches built in recent decades but without any real liturgical understanding. Sometimes it is precisely in such

[1] J. A. Jungmann, S. J. *The Mass of the Roman Rite,* Engl. translation, London 1958.

182

cases that particularly convincing solutions are found. They will be the results of planning and construction which are in harmony with pastoral work and which, like it, always make their start from a given situation.

The position of the altar should therefore be central, in the sense of being visible from every seat in the church, dominating the whole area, and drawing attention towards itself. For this it is essential that it should stand at a certain height, but not so high as to lose the necessary contact with the congregation. A sanctuary like a stage with innumerable steps leading up to it reduces, even degrades, the congregation to passive participation. Where an elevation of this type is necessary for the altar to be visible, the church has been wrongly planned (generally on too large a scale) as far as its chief purpose, the living celebration of the Eucharist, is concerned.

We must also guard against any arbitrary enlarging of the actual altar itself in order to make it stand out. It does not do to decide the dimensions of the altar from, for example, its proportion to the choir or to the whole church. The size of the altar should not be determined by the layout or by the design of the intended church building but rather the other way round. It is rather the chalice and paten which are to lie on the altar and the priest who has to celebrate there that should dictate its size. Chalice and paten should not be lost to view on an expanse of altar; the celebrant should not look a small helpless figure in front of its vast dimensions. It should be borne in mind that up to the eleventh century altar-tables did not in general exceed the size of just over nine square feet. We should be satisfied with a width of about five to six feet. It can be equally deep – the depth should in any case not be too small.

But how then can the altar be given its proper prominence? First of all, as has been said already, by raising it moderately above the level of the rest of the church, just sufficiently for it to be visible from all sides. To achieve this, of course, adequate lighting, both during the day and by artificial light, is necessary. If possible the latter should be the sort where the source of light itself is concealed. Windows behind the altar, especially those which come down low, are often a drawback as far as the real impact of the altar is concerned.

Inside the church there should be a special altar precinct which must be at least one step higher than the rest of the church. But this should not be, as it were, tacked on to the main part, from outside since that would impede the link with the congregation. This part can be given further emphasis by a slight rail which naturally should not have the dividing aspect of a roodscreen. It can at the same time serve as the place for the distribution of Communion. More important, however, than the difference in level or the rail are the proportions of the free space surrounding the altar. It must have open access from all sides, must emphasize the altar's dignity and be kept free of everything superfluous and unsuitable.

One very appropriate way of accentuating the altar is by having a ciborium, an independent canopy above the altar, as we can see it in St. Peter's and in other ancient churches in Rome; the Vatican Church at the Brussels Exhibition had one too. In addition candlesticks can give a relatively small altar greater importance, if they are not put on it, but placed beside and around it.

Regarding the design of the altar nothing will be said here; that is a matter for the architect and artist who knows that he is dealing not with an ordinary simple table but with a sacred, sacrificial table. It should be borne in mind that it is not only the *mensa* that is permissible as the place for the cavity or sepulchre, to contain the sacred relics. Much depends on the choice of the right stone. We should refuse to make do with the altar trunk merely being faced with real stone and having an inner core in brick or concrete. Materials, design and furnishings should all give the impression of being sacred and sober, noble and splendid, not rough and ready nor yet frivolous and fanciful; no lace on the altar-cloths, for example. Fortunately no-one today thinks of giving the altar a reredos or even massed candles or in any way turning it into a mere base for statues. It is, in addition, more suitable for the altar-cloths to cover the whole surface of the altar and not just a small area at the front.

Where the wall behind the altar is high and bare, without windows, there is the problem of whether and how it should be decorated. In Protestant churches a simple cross of suitable size seems to be considered as an appropriate declaration of faith. In our churches one often gains the impression of a makeshift approach to this problem. It is essential that we act with circumspection in this matter, for otherwise a great deal may be spoiled. In some circumstances a "blank wall" may be a better expression for the divine sphere – beyond the threshold which the altar is felt to be – than any picture. A parish can gradually grow to an understanding of this. In any case, if the construction of the body of the church and the sanctuary does not clearly proclaim the central importance of the Eucharistic mystery, this neglect cannot be made good by any pictorial representation. At the very least the mural should not distract the mind from it, like a new type of retable, by presenting either

185

some sacred narrative or a depiction of the church's patron saint, for example. The canopied altar has the advantage of preventing this problem even from arising.

Up till now we have only been discussing the main altar of the church. Even where the regulations do not require it, it should always be consecrated and not, as it were, just a covering for an altar-stone. There is good sense even today in having only one altar in the church, as was so greatly esteemed in earlier ages. Today, in any case, we would only have "side-altars" for the celebration of the Eucharist and not as accessories for some devotion or other. There are relatively few churches nowadays in which Masses have to be said simultaneously, because of the large number of priests. But it is an advantage if there is a side chapel with its own altar which can be used for Masses when there is only a small congregation as on weekdays.

The celebration of Mass facing the people is a form of Eucharistic celebration that deserves respect by reason of its long standing and that is inherently justifiable and legitimate. Today, however, it would hardly seem to have the same urgency as a few years ago. It demands exterior as well as interior conditions which are rarely present and which are difficult to create. The possibility of having this form of celebration should, however, be left open in every new church building, if not at the main altar then at least in a side chapel.

An altar of between five and six feet long requires a smaller Missal than one which is twice the size. Unfortunately, there are as yet no missals of a suitable size (16 inches wide when open, at the most) with sufficiently large type. Perhaps some day someone will begin making them in two volumes, like the four volumes of the Breviary we have had for so long. It would be far from superfluous to provide a place of honour inside the sanctuary for the Gospel Book.

The Cross can stand on the altar or hang above it, it can have a base or be a processional cross; or, as a substitute, a suitable cross can be painted on the wall behind the altar. Not all these possibilities should be adopted at the same time. Anything which is repeated two or three times over quickly loses its impact. Similarly, there should be no attempt to augment the dignified row of four or six candlesticks by an arrangement of numerous candles: here, as so often, the fewer the more impressive. On special occasions, such as the Easter Vigil, the whole sanctuary or the whole church can be radiant with candlelight; this does not, in any case, require increasing the number of altar-candles. If candles are burning elsewhere in the church, for example, in front of the statue of a saint, the pre-eminence of the altar should be clearly indicated by the size of its candles and candle-sticks.

The same principle applies to flower decorations: they may be used as a means of giving special honour to the altar but they should never be accumulated indiscriminately nor, placed in unsuitable vases.

The cross and candlesticks are the altar's accessories and should be subordinate to it and its purpose. It is not in accordance with this order of importance for the cross to be so big that it dominates the sanctuary or the whole church.

The Credence Table is a necessary but minor accessory in the sanctuary. It can have a very distracting effect, if not enough thought has been given beforehand to where it can be placed unobtrusively. Possibly this can be avoided by only having a special table for it at solemn Masses on feastdays and otherwise using a shelf just large enough to carry the cruets.

187

Part of the altar furnishings is the constantly burning Sanctuary Lamp. It can hang from the ceiling, rest on a stand (this is usually less beautiful) or be fixed to a holder on the wall. It is not admissible to put it on the altar itself. Care should be taken with its size and fittings to see that it does not come too much into the foreground or become a focal point. It is, after all, merely an indication of something else, which should itself provide the focal point.

The Altar-Cards should be readable yet not too large in relation to the rest. Under no circumstances should they be left on the altar till the next day; this also applies to the book-rest, the bowl for the ablutions and similar objects. Nor should all kinds of utensils be placed on the altar during the celebration.

Few features of church planning have been more widely discussed in recent years than the specifications for the tabernacle. In the end it has been agreed that the tabernacle should, in principle, not be put on an altar other than the high altar. Yet now as before a side-altar can be considered for this purpose in particular circumstances. In new buildings, however, the tabernacle must stand on one altar and be firmly fixed to it. Here we can see the fulfilment of one important demand of the liturgical revival: that the reservation and adoration of the Eucharist should not be separated from the celebration of the Eucharist. To set up an altar for the sacrament in the middle nave of the church behind the high altar (which was an arrangement considered for a while as the solution) is a course which now also meets with many objections.

We can find no example from the past to guide us as regards the design of the tabernacle, since its history does not go back as far as the romanesque and pre-romanesque period, the

188

styles of which are in many respects closer to us. Gothic and baroque designs have of course not been "canonized"; they are useless for a modern altar. There is, indeed, very little to say about it, except that it should remind us that it is "a shrine for the reservation of precious objects". Its size will be determined, on the one hand, by its purpose: simply the reserving of the small hosts needed to make up any discrepancy (since at each Mass there should be consecration for the participants) and for the Communion of the sick, as well as to keep the monstrance with the Exposition host; and, on the other hand, by the necessity of giving it the emphasis appropriate to its importance; naturally this must be in the right proportion to the altar.

The tabernacle should be wholly gold-plated inside or lined with silk; the former is recommended since it is both more distinguished and more practical. It is unnecessary to keep a *corporale* in it, since in accordance with its blessing the tabernacle is equal to the pyx in serving for the preservation of the species.

The throne prescribed for the solemn exposition of the Blessed Sacrament should not be fixed permanently to the tabernacle or altar, but put up only when required.

21

Altar Furnishings

1. Chalice and Paten

THE new approach to the essential nature of the sacrifice of the Mass must sooner or later arouse dissatisfaction with Mass vessels which fall short of their essential purpose. As far back as the Gothic period baroque elaborations on the stem of the chalice had begun. The cup gradually lost its significant form. The decorative designs of succeeding eras ran riot over base, stem and cup alike. Nineteenth century historicism attempted – with little success – to copy the formal perfection of earlier vessels. Such imitations are not for us if we are concerned with liturgical revival in every sphere.

For the last thirty years there have been tentative experiments, some of which are still uncertain even today, although their aim is well-defined. The trend towards Romanesque designs is due less to imitation than to a spiritual affinity; and this is true also where church furnishings are concerned. It should be the intention, when new designs are created, to make the cup, stem and base into one harmonious whole, while preserving the importance of the cup as the receptacle for the mystery of our faith and yet avoiding exaggerated one-sidedness. The chalice is an entity which has either static or dynamic form; that is, it is either

190

in repose hiding the mystery or else showing the mystery forth by its upward sweep.

If the base on a chalice is over-small, it endangers its stability, while an over-thick stem makes it difficult to take and keep hold of the chalice between index-finger and thumb helped by the other fingers. There is no need, however, for exaggerated concern, since the "new" chalices are considerably less tall than those customary in previous centuries and are therefore less likely to be knocked over; in addition their centre of gravity is lower, especially when the smaller bases are made heavier by having metal weights put inside them. As in the case of the new semi-circular chasubles, a certain heaviness should be welcomed as a symbol of the celebrant's priestly burden; indeed, he will handle the chalice and even go about the whole celebration of the Mass more carefully than when everything is so very handy and easy to manipulate. The customary knob on the stem has undergone new modifications, some of which have modified it practically out of existence, for instance, stones set in the foot and so on; our short modern stems do not, in any case, need the knob as much as the over-elaborate ones of earlier designs.

Apart from the precious metals the materials which are available today are: enamel or ivory (with a gold rim and inlay) for the cup; in addition to these, rock-crystal and ebony for the stem and base. There must be a very definite shape so that the chalice remains a whole, even when it is of various materials, and does not look as if it had been simply "knocked-up". Only then the variety in material becomes ornamental. There are pitfalls in "additional" ornamentation here as in the case of vestments and it should always be subordinate to the shape and material of the chalice. The temptation ought to be resisted to show off with the use of precious stones, pearls, ivory, cloisonné work and inlays on enamel, engraving and filigree work.

The paten should owe its beauty to its shape and to the nobly worked material of which it is made and can do without any special ornamentation. It should not be too small, so that it is suitable for the gesture of oblation.

2. Ciborium

The customary *ciboria* have altered their basic shape so much in the course of centuries that up till now we have been distributing the Holy Food from drinking vessels. The pyxes of earlier times, which in the Middle Ages were often raised like a monstrance on a base and stem (with a knob), have in recent centuries been wrongly thought of as chalices and have then been provided with a lid and a veil.

There have been attempts recently to develop new designs, in the form of patens for consecration without a lid (only covered with the pall when not intended for keeping the sacred hosts); in the shape of plates with a grip on the rims or a handle underneath; or dishes on a very low base fitting easily into the flat of the left hand and held firm by cupping the fingers. The last-mentioned method has the great advantage that the dish's centre of gravity is over the middle of the hand, while that of the plate held by its rim is far to the right of the hand, which can sometimes be very cumbersome; in addition, large plates carried in this way obstruct the priest's view of the communicants. The centre of the plate or dish should be slightly depressed so that the last few hosts can be picked up easily.

192

When used for reservation these dishes should be silver- or gold-plated at least on the inside. The lid could be ornamented, but the rim of the dishes should if possible be left free with regard to the purification, which is generally dry in the case of simple consecration patens, as in that of the chalice-type patens. Any of the sacred hosts left over should be placed before Mass in other *ciboria* in the tabernacle. Then if the hosts are insufficient, they would have to be taken from the above-mentioned *ciboria*. Any increase in the number of hosts kept in this way must be carefully avoided, perhaps by using them up in a chapel where hosts are not consecrated at every Mass.

3. Putting out the Hosts

The encyclical *Mediator Dei* stipulates that the hosts distributed at Communion should be consecrated at the same celebration of the Mass. The sacrificial meal at a sacrificial celebration should not come from another Mass which has already taken place. How can this be done meaningfully, except by having the faithful themselves lay out the hosts for the Mass on to a paten as they enter the Church before the beginning of Mass? An understanding of this was for a long time hindered by the traditional practice, until suddenly it was appreciated and, having been wisely put into practice, is unlikely to be given up either by the priest or by his parish who, through his efforts, are aware of its meaning.

It is not difficult to present this method of putting out the hosts to the faithful as an act of active participation and co-operation in preparing the supper of the Mass. It must be granted that the gifts of bread and wine are no longer directly presented by the faithful and are therefore no longer "their" direct offerings. But seen in conjunction with the collection of money for the needs of the parish, the hosts laid out by the faithful take on a deeper symbolic meaning both for our devotion to God and our incorporation in Christ, who has chosen the form of bread under which to remain with us. Nor does it matter that our gifts are, in a material sense, almost worthless, if we know how to re-interpret these gifts again and again as basic "human" symbols and at the same time can play our part in translating what they mean into real terms in relation to the will of God and the expectation of our neighbour. It would be helpful if the hosts we use looked more like bread, even if our new patens had to be bigger and deeper. Patience with the people and a love of making the Mass accessible to them will create new and good habits in spite of technical and psychological difficulties. At the Offertory the acolytes should bear to the altar, through the midst of the faithful, not only the hosts put out ready by the congregation, but also wine and water.

Putting out the hosts demands light handling and, at the same time, hygienic safeguards. The hosts should be placed on a dish (or plate) which is covered with a white cloth, so that they do not slip off if they are picked up with the help of small shovels, since the taut cloth gives easily way when it is touched with the shovels. The shovels must be wider at the end than the individual hosts, sharp, perhaps a little pointed in the middle, and the sides should have a small rim; the handle should not be too heavy and should be the same width throughout, convenient for holding with the thumb and index-finger. Even in large churches the putting out of the hosts on to the paten can be carried out smoothly and without delays if here are two shovels to every

194

plate. The shovels are used to put the hosts into a polished metal dish, then they are carried, covered by a pall (for reasons of hygiene) to the altar by an acolyte. The hosts left over are kept covered in the same way until the next Mass. The hosts are handed over at the Epistle side and poured into the consecration paten by the celebrant, if he prefers not to use this as the dish in which they are put out and presented. The fact that if this is done the tabernacle is not opened during Mass makes obvious to the people the unity of the sacrifice.

4. Ostensoria

Used as it is for the Eucharist, the Monstrance belongs to altar and tabernacle. Customary are the forms of a cluster of metallic rays or a tower, but other shapes such as the tree of life and the standard of Christ are being used. Today, rock-crystal, enamel and ivory are fashioned to better effect than previously. Decorative embellishments and stones must be strictly subordinated to the cult. All ornamentation should be at once plain, precious and simple.

5. The Altar Cross

The fact that we have returned to earlier models for our altars has resulted to a large extent in the re-designing of the altar-cross; frequently now a processional cross with a long staff is used and is carried ahead at the Introit of High Mass and placed as the standard of Christ on the "hill of salvation" behind (or in front of) the altar, where Golgotha is about to be realized. Thus this cross has regained the significance it had in early Christian centuries, decorated with precious stones, enamel or ivory on a background of precious metal or other material. This regard for the cross and its crucifix emphasizes the glory of the risen Lord, who with his followers renews his dedication to the Father. The image of the Lord is that of the victor who rises, free of thorns and nails, from the cross to the Father. There are representations (for example, in inlaid ivory on a precious cross) which leave it open whether it is the Christ child, the Crucified or the Risen Lord. (The image of Christ as it emerges from the Canon of the Mass is a great help for an instruction on the Mass.) Such portrayals were typical of Romanesque art and later, too, there were many representations of this aspect of his glory. A portrayal exclusively of Christ's Passion at no time corresponded to the full reality of the Mass. Modern portrayals of Christ, in which his features are not depicted in detail seek to avoid such historical representations and to give expression to the ineffability of his fullness and his mystery. The celebrant must patiently open the minds and the senses of his congregation, as well as his own, to this image of Christ as he really is in the Mass, unless he wishes to persist in the sort of portrayals that mean nothing to us today. Altar-crosses without a staff can hang free above the altar or else they have a small base and stand on the mensa. They should always match the altar in design and material. The back of these crosses should be no less carefully designed than the front.

6. Candlesticks

The altar candlesticks should be in keeping with the cross, especially since their candles symbolize the Lord of the Mass. Simple table altars should have shallow candlesticks (bowls) with short, thick candles. Tall candlesticks with big candles on this sort of altar often inadvertently look as though they are trying to act as a substitute for a missing retable. The more we feel the altar to be the Lord's table for the sacrificial meal, the more easily will we, priest and people, learn to prefer the altar-table with low candlesticks and few rather than a great many flowers. The furnishings and decoration of a Gothic or baroque altar must necessarily be different and in keeping with the style; but the altars in these styles have almost completely lost what should be their essential character. An effective way of decorating the altar is to place candlesticks and vases of flowers on the floor on each side of the altar.

In spite of the fact that it stands independently, the candle-stick for the Paschal Candle should fit in with the altar and sanctuary as regards its design and the metal in which it is made.

For the Sanctuary Lamp, particularly fine glass should be chosen, with a simple design for the metal parts.

7. *Altar Cloths*

These should cover the *mensa,* hanging down on all sides. Preferably they should not be decorated with lace or appliqué work. Embroidery or lace at the front of the altar ruin its proportions or spoil the style and colour of the frontal. On great feasts it is permissible to cover all the altar with a large richly woven cloth as a decoration. The linen cloths are placed on top of it and, in this case, the tabernacle is left free.

8. Altar Cards

These are essential aids rather than an altar decoration, and for this reason are better left flat rather than standing up. For the same reason they should be modest in size and design.

9. Liturgical Books

The Missal should not be too brightly coloured for fear of clashing with vestments or furnishings. There should be no false ostentation, no excessive intricacy in the embossing of the leather cover, no multi-coloured bindings; leather markers of the same colour as the binding; the edges preferably in a pastel colour rather than, for instance, bright red. Perhaps we should try to introduce new bindings ornamented with enamels, precious stones, or filigree work for the book of Lessons or for the Holy Week book. This would emphasize strikingly the importance of the proclamation of the Word and the celebration of the Easter mysteries.

If it is at all possible the rest for the Missal on altars which do not have a reredos should be as low as possible and covered in a neutral material if not in natural leather. Instead of a rest, cushions with some kind of stiffening are also used, so that the Missal can be carried more easily by the younger altar-servers.

22

Co-operation Between Priests and Artists

ANYONE building a house for himself has certain preconceived ideas and will try, in a series of discussions, to bring these ideas into harmony with those of his architect. Even if he has unbounded confidence in his architect, the latter must know how many rooms there are to be, whether one garage is desired or two, and what are the wife's wishes regarding the kitchen.

In the same way a parish-priest who has to build or restore a church cannot make the whole thing easy for himself by leaving everything to the architect. He must have clear and definite ideas about the functions and the structure of the inside of a church; that is, when thinking it over, he must start from the function of the altar and the sacred acts which take place there. If his architect is an experienced church builder, then there will be no differences of opinion here; if, however, he is still an inexperienced man, the parish-priest has the duty of imparting the essential fundamentals to him, either by intensive discussions or perhaps by means of an instructive book on church architecture; otherwise they will be constantly at cross-purposes. Every true artist will not only be grateful for such advice but will even be eager to learn anything useful from the "expert"; for perhaps far too little was told him about the nature of the liturgy during his period of training.

199

We might recall the fruitful exchanges between artists and theologians in the great churches and also in the paintings of the Counter Reformation period in Europe. The brothers Asam, for instance, would never have achieved their magnificent, profound, and artistic expressions of faith without a fundamental knowledge of theology, which they gained not in schools but in conversations. Today when so many standards have been lost and so many traditions torn up, artists are looking for guidance. Here the theologian could and should show himself a true friend and assistant.

The parish-priest, therefore, should not leave the artist to himself. It is equally true, however, that he should not play a dictatorial rôle. He has a right to discuss and even to decide questions of the ideal fundamentals, but he clearly has a duty to hold back where questions of design, proportion, and detail are concerned. He must always remember the artist's ability is a talent, which is also subordinate to a personal responsibility. He must respect the decisions of genius, whose sphere he enters here. The artist must feel that he has freedom; for he is more than a workman who carries out everything according to his directions. He has the gift of filling the functional with the breath of living poetry, with the radiance of beauty, which is not at all the same thing as making it "look nice". The priest would not accept instruction on the nature of the Mass or the *communio sanctorum* from the artist (for it may be, as not infrequently happens, that he is confronted with a "lay theologian"); he cannot then expect the artist to accept instruction on what is beautiful, modern, or in good taste.

In questions of so-called artistic taste the theologian must be the more cautious, the stronger the personality of the artist working with him. Of course, he will have to point out one limitation on the artist; as pastor of souls he even has a duty to point it out: "edification" in the Pauline sense. He should induce even the reluctant and highhanded artist to create his art for the people. He should not foist on him a copy of what is traditional, a dull "generally intelligible" design, but he will have to convince him that to make something for a private person or for his own personal pleasure is something quite different, and that he must take upon himself, in his work, a service to the people of the parish.

The problem which very easily arises here can best be dealt with if the artist – and I am not now speaking only of the architect – puts forward several plans and, if need be, works hard on these plans, until a solution is reached which, without being a bad compromise, fulfils the desires of the priest as well as his own.

Architects have a not entirely unmerited reputation for not having "both feet on the ground", that is, they are not sufficiently aware of the practical necessities, or else they are far too ready to sacrifice these to aesthetic considerations. Here the priest who is commissioning the architect must be on the watch and, when necessary, inexorable; for what use to the priest is the most beautiful building if it cannot be ventilated or the heating doesn't function properly or too little thought has been given to the materials and workmanship. It may sound unpleasant, but it is true, that a church is first and foremost a functional building and we have, above all, to make everything serve the desired purpose as perfectly as possible. It is by this subordination that the artist must prove that he is willing to be a servant and not a master. His task is to build a house for the parish and not a memorial to his own glory.

With the other artists too, who are doing work for the church (goldsmiths, weavers and seamstresses, painters and sculptors), the priest should start up fruitful discussions. It is irresponsible to commission a painting or sculpture without any forethought or without communicating and exchanging ideas with the artist; and I consider that this also holds good for the extensive field of altar furnishings, which is in the middle of new developments. In discovering the essential bases for the artist's task in the riches of biblical, mystical and philosophical tradition, the theologian has not indicated the routes art should take, but he has suggested them; he has set free these men who are seeking God – for all true artists are seeking God – set them free from the disastrous vicious circle, in which art is only a reflection or presentation of the artist's self and the artist sees himself as the pivot of everything. To set free these men for true service is itself a service of brotherly love.

Finally, I should like to point out what should have been pointed out at the beginning. Precisely because nowadays there is a greater number of artists who have their roots firmly in the life of the Church, who are seeking the truth with their whole heart, theologians should at long last embrace them with open arms. It is still thought of as a hobby of aesthetically-minded or artistically educated priests to give commissions to well-known or aspiring artists; very many of our fellow priests still think it is easiest and cheapest to take into consideration the offers of some factory or other; it is still considered impossible to pass over a so-called local genius. As far as altar furnishings are concerned, it is shocking what sums are thrown away year after year in order to obtain some really horrible manufactured article. It is not true that artists work at prohibitive prices. On the contrary, in many cases it happens that the work of a real artist is cheaper than something mass-produced in a factory. But quite apart from the price question (which can, in any case, be solved quite simply by waiting to save up the difference) should not the basic rule for the house of God be: Only the best is good enough? Anyone who has acquired even one important work of art can say how it becomes more beautiful year by year and how great is its power of giving joy to the people. It is for the priests and theologians to mould our people, to be, as it were, the sculptors of their spiritual life. It is not only with words that they are formed but also, and perhaps even more so, with statues or pictures, which are looked at again and again and which become part of their world and inspiring environment.

We all know both from past and present experience how difficult it is for artists, especially the young ones, to earn any sort of living at all. If more priests could make the decision to work with them, which means they must seek them out and talk with them, then a good deal of their hardship would be overcome. For they want to see their life as a service to the Church. But what can they do if the Church does not call them into her service? They have received their talents from God and want to use them to God's honour and glory. But what can they do if we pass over these talents without heeding them and go on being satisfied with false glitter?

Much has been done already: exhibitions of ecclesiastical art have been arranged, here and there fine churches have been built, works of art have been placed inside and outside some of our churches. But these first steps must be followed by many others. It is often said that art is for the people. This is certainly nowhere more meaningful and more urgent than in the Church.